Judy Garton-Sprenger • Philip Prowse

with Helena Gomm and Catherine Smith

BODY AND MIND

1 It doesn't matter

1 Reading

Read and complete the text with these words.

ate believe cereal contain depends have
healthy lower need prove reduce skip

An apple a day keeps the doctor away.
Maybe, but they are much (**1**) _____ in vitamin C than, say, oranges or even bananas. However, apples are fat-free and they (**2**) _____ things which support the action of vitamins and (**3**) _____ the chances of heart disease.

Carrots help you see at night.
It (**4**) _____. If you already (**5**) _____ a problem with seeing at night, eating carrots may help. Eyes (**6**) _____ vitamin A to see in the dark, and carrots contain something called beta carotene, which the body turns into vitamin A.

Oranges stop you from getting colds.
People (**7**) _____ this because oranges contain vitamin C, but there is nothing to (**8**) _____ that vitamin C stops people from getting colds. But it's very important to get enough vitamin C—we need about 30 mg a day to be (**9**) _____.

Breakfast is the most important meal of the day.
This may well be true. A recent survey of 500 schoolchildren showed that those who had (**10**) _____ for breakfast before an exam got better results than those who (**11**) _____ nothing. Another survey showed that people who (**12**) _____ breakfast are more likely to be overweight.

2 Simple present and present progressive

Complete with the simple present or present progressive of the verbs.

1 "I _____ (enjoy) doing this project with you."
  "I _____ (agree). I am, too."
2 "_____ you _____ (feel) like going out this evening?"
  "I _____ (not know). It _____ (depend)."
3 "Look at the girl over there. I think she _____ (laugh) at you."
  "It _____ (not matter). I _____ (know) I look silly in this hat!"
4 "Oh, the band _____ (play) my favorite song!"
  "I _____ (like) this song, too. I _____ (think) it _____ (sound) great."
5 "Why _____ you _____ (look) at me like that?"
  "I _____ (not understand) what you _____ (mean)!"
6 "Look—a woman in white _____ (walk) up the stairs!"
  "Nonsense! I _____ (not believe) in ghosts."

UNIT 1

3 Simple past and past progressive

Complete with the simple past or past progressive of the verbs.

1 Last night we .... (watch) TV when the phone .... (ring). It was my brother and he .... (sound) upset.

2 The soup .... (taste) better than it .... (smell). I really .... (like) it.

3 I .... (see) him at the party yesterday, but I .... (not recognize) him at first.

4 Sorry I .... (call) at a bad time—I .... (not realize) you .... (have) dinner.

5 She .... (promise) to keep in touch while she .... (travel) in Mexico.

4 Vocabulary

Complete the sentences with these words.

diet digest exaggerate junk food
nightmare portion protein scientific

1 I slept badly last night because I had a terrible ....

2 Fish is very good for you—it contains lots of ....

3 A healthy .... includes plenty of fruit and vegetables.

4 The food wasn't so bad—don't .... !

5 Some people say that cheese is difficult to ....

6 It's not a good idea to eat too much .... , like French fries and cookies.

7 .... research has shown that iron-rich food helps you concentrate.

8 I'd like a small .... of potatoes.

5 Vocabulary

Match the words in list A with the words in list B and write six compound nouns.

A	B	
1 balanced	fruit	1 *balanced diet*
2 dried	water	2
3 food	juice	3
4 fruit	diet	4
5 tap	decay	5
6 tooth	label	6

6 Vocabulary

Find 11 words for food and drink in the word square.

V	B	X	R	W	M	E	A	T	C
E	M	I	L	K	A	D	C	U	O
G	C	C	F	O	R	G	E	L	O
E	A	H	S	U	G	A	R	J	K
T	R	E	I	F	A	Q	E	U	I
A	R	E	G	R	R	H	A	I	E
B	O	S	C	U	I	T	L	C	A
L	T	E	Y	I	N	W	O	E	T
E	B	U	T	T	E	R	F	K	E

7 Vocabulary

Compare the words in list A with the words in list B. Write *S* if they have almost the same meaning, *O* if they are opposites, and *G* if A is more general than B.

	A	B	
1	reduce	increase	*O*
2	type	kind	
3	fact	fiction	
4	seem	appear	
5	drink	juice	
6	indicate	show	

8 Pronunciation

Write the number of syllables and mark the stress.

■
acidic *3*   advertising ......   balanced ......

emphasize ......   exaggerate ......   margarine ......

mineral ......   scientific ......   unhealthy ......   vitamin ......

9 Pronunciation

Do they rhyme (✓) or not (✗)?

1	cost	most	✗
2	diet	quiet	
3	fruit	boot	
4	juice	choose	
5	label	table	
6	taste	fast	

Extension Make a list of all the things you ate yesterday. Then make a food word map with sections for fruit and vegetables, meat, cereals, dairy products, and junk food. Put in the things on your list. How many other words can you add?

3

1 BODY AND MIND

2 What's it for?

The green machine

Doing the laundry can keep you in shape! Alex Gadsden, an avid cyclist, has come up with a great invention—an exercise bike which is also a machine for washing clothes. By running his washing machine, Alex can do exercise, do the housework, and save energy all at the same time.

The 29-year-old starts each day by cycling for 45 minutes. His washing machine uses 25 liters of water per wash. The clothes are first washed in half the water for 30 minutes. After draining the clothes, Alex puts the rest of the water into the machine. He then cycles for another 15 minutes, before taking the clean clothes out of the machine and putting them out to dry.

Alex finally finished building his washing machine after working on it in the evenings for about 20 weeks. He says: "After using the machine for two weeks, I already feel healthier." He added: "There's definitely a future for it."

1 Reading

Read the text. Then match the numbers 1–6 with the correct phrase a–f.

1 20   a the number of minutes he cycles after adding the second half of the water
2 29   b the number of weeks it took to build the machine
3 25   c the number of minutes it takes to do the first part of the wash
4 15   d the number of liters of water he uses for each wash
5 30   e the number of minutes Alex cycles every morning
6 45   f Alex's age

2 Gerund as subject

Rewrite the sentences with a gerund as subject.

1 It isn't difficult to make Spaghetti Carbonara.
   Making Spaghetti Carbonara isn't difficult.

2 It takes about four minutes to boil an egg.

3 It's sometimes hard to get up in the morning.

4 It's fun to sleep under the stars.

5 It felt great to win the soccer game.

6 It wasn't easy to get tickets for the concert.

7 It was exciting to meet the band.

8 It seemed strange to be at home alone.

4

UNIT 1

3 by + gerund

Complete the sentences with *by* + gerund using these phrases.

> call 911   follow a recipe   press this button
> set your alarm clock   use a dictionary
> ~~wear a "sleep inducer"~~

1 You can get to sleep *by wearing a "sleep inducer."*
2 You can learn to cook a new dish
3 You can make sure you wake up in the morning
4 You start the computer
5 You can find out what a word means
6 You contact the emergency services

4 for + gerund

What are the items for? Write sentences using these phrases.

> carry water   do calculations   iron clothes   listen to music
> ~~lock the door~~   open bottles   serve soup   tell the time

1 *It's for locking the door.*

5

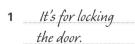

2

6

3

7

4

8

5 after/before + participle clause

Complete the sentences with *after* or *before* + ...-*ing*.

1 You celebrate _____ (pass) your exams.
2 You look at a map _____ (start) a trip.
3 You set the alarm _____ (go) to sleep.
4 You feel thirsty _____ (eat) salt.
5 You dry your hair _____ (wash) it.
6 You get dressed _____ (wake up).

6 Vocabulary

Match these verbs with the kitchen equipment.

> beat   boil   ~~chop~~   drain   fry   stir

1 *chop*   4

2   5

3   6

7 Vocabulary

Match the words in list A with the words in list B and write five compound nouns.

	A	B		
1	cheese	screw	1	*cheese grater*
2	coffee	pan	2	
3	cork	maker	3	
4	sauce	grater	4	
5	can	opener	5	

8 Pronunciation

Match the rhyming words.

1 bowl   a door
2 drawer   b fault
3 grate   c metal
4 kettle   d roll
5 salt   e straight

> **Extension** Think of a new gadget that could help you in your daily life, such as a robot that does homework. Write a paragraph describing it.

BODY AND MIND

3 When people expect to get better ...

1 Reading

Read the text and complete it with the gerund form of these verbs.

be climb drive fly get live look panic scream see swim travel use work

Many people try (1) .... alternative medicine to treat a phobia—when they are extremely afraid of something for no logical reason.

For example, some people are scared of cars and hate (2) ...., others never risk (3) .... by plane because they hate (4) .... so much. Some people can't face (5) .... up lots of steps, and others avoid (6) .... into elevators. Some people can't stand (7) .... at snakes, and others can't help (8) .... at the top of their voice when they see a spider. One of the most modern phobias is technophobia, suffered by people who dislike (9) .... with new technology, especially computers!

Sometimes a phobia is a reaction to a past experience, even to a movie. Many people stopped (10) .... in the ocean because of the movie *Jaws*. One woman remembered (11) .... Alfred Hitchcock's movie *The Birds* when she was young, with the result that she kept (12) .... when she saw birds. She couldn't imagine (13) .... without her phobia, but now, after acupuncture treatment, she doesn't mind (14) .... near birds at all.

2 Verb + infinitive

Complete with the infinitive of these verbs.

be get go help hurt quit study take try

1 Acupuncture appears .... some people with back pain.
2 I expected the needles ...., but they didn't really.
3 I wouldn't agree .... part in a medical trial.
4 He's pretending .... sick because he doesn't want .... to school.
5 If you want to be a doctor, you must be prepared .... for a long time.
6 She hopes .... better after taking the medicine.
7 Would you like .... alternative medicine?
8 My brother decided .... drinking coffee last month.

3 Verb + gerund or infinitive

Complete with the gerund or infinitive of the verbs.

1 I remember .... (feel) excited the first time I went on a plane.
2 I don't mind .... (fly), but I'd prefer .... (take) the train.
3 He was trying .... (go) to sleep, but he couldn't manage .... (relax).
4 If you want .... (get) to sleep, try .... (read) a boring book!
5 Don't forget .... (take) your pills—you need .... (keep) (take) them regularly.
6 I'll never forget .... (see) my baby brother for the first time.
7 Remember .... (put) the meat in the oven—and don't forget .... (take) it out after 45 minutes.

6

UNIT 1

4 Prepositions

Complete with these prepositions.

> about for of to with

1 Doctors are responsible .... taking care of patients.
2 Herbalists treat their patients .... natural remedies.
3 The effect .... the drug is to reduce pain.
4 She told me .... her visit to the doctor.
5 An aspirin is a pill .... headaches.
6 I hate the thought .... having an operation.
7 What's your reaction .... the latest news?

5 Crossword

Complete the crossword puzzle and find the extra word ↓.

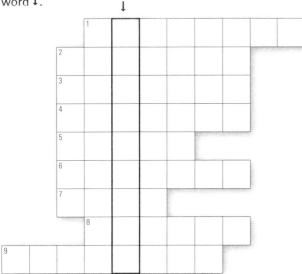

1 Place where nurses work.
2 The first synthetic drug.
3 They are used in acupuncture.
4 Person who carries out operations.
5 You use this part of your head to think.
6 Someone who is receiving medical treatment.
7 Your body feels this when you are hurt.
8 Person who gives medical treatment.
9 Noun formed from *sick*.

6 Vocabulary

Match the words in list A with the words in list B and write five compound nouns.

	A	B		
1	alternative	ache	1	*alternative medicine*
2	general	remedy	2	
3	head	medicine	3	
4	open-heart	anesthetic	4	
5	natural	surgery	5	

7 Vocabulary

Find words in the text on page 14 of the Student's Book which mean the opposite of these words.

1 at worst ....
2 dangerous ....
3 forget ....
4 health ....
5 nervous ....
6 synthetic ....
7 negative ....
8 fake ....

8 Pronunciation

Write these words under *sound* or *touch*.

> ~~amount~~ count country cousin doubt
> enough round thousand trouble young

/aʊ/ sound	/ʌ/ touch
amount	

9 Pronunciation

Write the number of syllables and mark the stress.

acupuncture *4*   alternative ......   anesthetic ......
experiment ......   individual ......   operation ......
placebo ......   popularity ......
reaction ......   remedy ......   surgeon ......   synthetic ......

> **Extension** Write a paragraph about a time when you were sick. What did you do? Who did you see? What medicines did you take?

7

1 BODY AND MIND

4 Integrated Skills

Discussing and correcting information

1 Reading

Read *Truth or Myth?* and match four of the statements 1–6 with paragraphs A–D.

1 Garlic reduces the risk of heart disease.
2 Juggling is good for the brain.
3 Eating oranges can stop you from getting colds.
4 Sitting too close to a television is bad for your eyes.
5 If you get cold, you risk catching a cold.
6 Reading in poor light can damage your eyes.

Truth or Myth?

A _____

This is a (**1**) _____. It won't damage your eyes, (**2**) _____ it might give you a headache. The (**3**) _____ thing is to watch TV at a distance that feels comfortable. But watching too much TV can be a bad idea. In (**4**) _____, research shows that children who (**5**) _____ spend more than 10 hours a week watching TV are more likely to be overweight, and slower to learn at school.

B _____

This (**6**) _____ to be true. Scientists have found that juggling balls for one minute every day can increase your brain (**7**) _____. Researchers in Germany carried out brain scans and found that certain areas of the brain had grown (**8**) _____ in people who practiced juggling. However, when they (**9**) _____ juggling, their brains went back to their (**10**) _____ size.

C _____

This is a (**11**) _____ belief, but scientists say there is nothing to (**12**) _____ that it's true. However, the use of this vegetable as a natural (**13**) _____ goes back to the Ancient Egyptians, and research shows that it can be an effective (**14**) _____ for coughs, sore throats, and upset stomachs, among other (**15**) _____. Unfortunately, many people dislike the smell, but you can take it in pill form.

D _____

The truth is that people get colds from viruses, not from being cold. (**16**) _____, keeping warm may help you to (**17**) _____ getting a cold. Researchers at Cardiff University's Common Cold Centre found that a fall in body temperature can (**18**) _____ cold viruses to become active. In a (**19**) _____, a group of people sat with their feet in (**20**) _____ of ice water for 20 minutes. A third of them developed colds in the next five days, compared to only 9 percent of another group who kept dry.

2 Vocabulary

Complete *Truth or Myth?* with these words.

although   appears   avoid   bowls   cause   common   fact   however   illnesses   larger
myth   normal   power   prove   regularly   remedy   sensible   stopped   treatment   trial

8

3 Crossword

Complete the crossword puzzle.

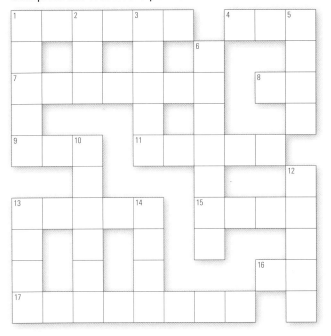

Across →
1. A tea… is for boiling water. (6)
4. When you cook pasta, … salt to the water. (3)
7. You can practice activities to … your memory. (7)
8. The Empire State Building is designed … a lightning conductor. (2)
9. We need to … five portions of fruit and vegetables a day. (3)
11. Opposite of *sensible*. (5)
13. A thick yellow liquid from the top of milk. (5)
15. Before frying the onions, … the oil in a frying pan. (4)
16. Some people hate getting … early in the morning. (2)
17. Opposite of *negative*. (8)

Down ↓
1. You use this to cut your food. (5)
2. In some countries, it isn't safe to drink … water. (3)
3. The bottle opener … like a key. (5)
5. Spaghetti Carbonara is an Italian … . (4)
6. Dried fruit and fresh fruit are equally … . (7)
10. Herbal medicine … illness with natural remedies. (6)
12. Experts recommend walking 10,000 … a day. (5)
13. Cut something into pieces. (4)
14. Vegetarians don't eat … . (4)

4 Writing

"Listening to loud music on MP3 players can damage your hearing: truth or myth?" Use the notes below to write a paragraph on this topic.

Millions own MP3 players
Music through headphones too loud → serious damage to ears
Continuous extremely loud noise → people become deaf
Warning sign: ringing/buzzing noise in ears
Research: over 25% of MP3 users listen to music at dangerous levels
Turn down MP3 players, listen for short periods with regular breaks

Noise levels
Quiet room at night—20 decibels
Ordinary conversation—60 decibels
Busy street—70 decibels
Risk to hearing—80 decibels
Some MP3 players at high volume—105 decibels
Plane taking off—110 decibels

LEARNER INDEPENDENCE

Using a dictionary

For each of these words from Unit 1, answer the questions below. Use an English–English dictionary to help you.

experiment   creative   damage   natural   sensible

- What does it mean? Is it a noun and/or a verb, or an adjective?
- How is it pronounced?
- What other words do you associate with it?
- What other words can you use with it?

Extensive reading

Read an English book and choose your favorite character. Write a description of the person and explain why you like him/her.

1 BODY AND MIND

Inspired EXTRA!

CONSOLIDATION

LESSON 1

Complete with the simple present or present progressive of the verbs.

1 Oranges _____ (contain) a lot of vitamin C.

2 "What _____ you _____ (eat)?" "Potato chips."

3 A balanced diet _____ (include) protein, minerals, and vitamins.

4 His breakfast _____ (consist) of cereal and a cup of coffee.

5 Mmm, something _____ (smell) good. What _____ you _____ (cook)?

6 You _____ (need) to eat something before you go school.

7 I _____ (not want) any French fries because I _____ (try) to lose weight.

8 Can she call you back? She _____ (take) a shower right now.

LESSON 2

Answer the questions using *for* and these phrases.

> carry things   cut things   ~~keep food cold~~   listen to music
> take pictures   wake you up   wash clothes   watch movies

1 What's a refrigerator for?
  It's for keeping food cold.

2 What's an alarm clock for?

3 What are scissors for?

4 What's a washing machine for?

5 What's an MP3 player for?

6 What's a DVD player for?

7 What's a basket for?

8 What's a camera for?

LESSON 3

Complete with the gerund or infinitive of the verbs.

1 Some people can't help _____ (eat) junk food.

2 I wouldn't want _____ (have) acupuncture.

3 Have you ever promised _____ (call) home regularly?

4 I don't remember _____ (see) anything unusual.

5 We asked them _____ (stop) _____ (talk).

6 Unfortunately they refused _____ (be) quiet.

7 Do you expect _____ (pass) the exam?

8 I've just finished _____ (do) this exercise!

LESSON 4

Match these words with their definitions.

1 belief ☐
2 daily ☐
3 obviously ☐
4 proof ☐
5 sensible ☐
6 strike ☐

a of course
b every day
c rational and practical
d evidence that something is true
e strong feeling that something is true
f hit

Spelling

Fill in the silent letters of these words from Unit 1.

1 althou_____   2 desi__n   3 dou__t   4 headac__e

5 h__art   6 __nife   7 li_____tning   8 mus__le

9 ni_____tmare   10 s__ientific   11 spag_____etti   12 surg_____on

Brainteaser

What's better than the best thing and worse than the worst thing?

Answer on page 25.

10

UNIT 1

EXTENSION

LESSON 1

Write eight sentences about your likes, dislikes, and opinions using eight different verbs from the box in exercise 5 on page 11 of the Student's Book.

LESSON 2

Answer the questions for yourself with *after/before ...-ing*.

1 When do you have dinner?

2 When do you take off your shoes?

3 When do you brush your teeth?

4 When do you take a shower?

5 When did you last drink a glass of water?

6 When did you last feel nervous?

7 When did you last watch TV?

8 When did you last wait in line?

LESSON 3

Complete these sentences for yourself using the infinitive and gerund in turn.

1 I must remember to
2 I don't remember
3 I didn't forget to
4 I'll never forget
5 I tried hard to
6 I'd like to try

LESSON 4

Look at exercise 4 on page 17 of the Student's Book and write a paragraph discussing one of the statements which you didn't choose in exercise 7.

Web watch

How much do you know about the food you like? Type "plastic fork diaries" into a search engine to find the *Plastic Fork Diaries* website. Go to *info bites* and click on *Show All Items*. Choose a topic and write a simple true/false quiz to test the other students in your class.

Spelling

Homophones are words which have the same sound but different spellings, for example /ðer/ = *their* and *there*. Write the homophones of these words. All the homophones are in Unit 1.

1 /eɪt/ ate
2 /ˈgreɪtər/ greater
3 /pleɪn/ plain
4 /roʊl/ role
5 /ˈweðər/ weather

Brainteaser

A man and his son were injured in a road accident. The boy was taken straight to the hospital in an ambulance. The surgeon at the hospital saw the boy and cried out, "That's my son!" How was this possible?

Answer on page 25.

11

1 Culture

Happiness and success
Teenage views on family, love, and money

> In a perfect world, people wouldn't base their idea of love on appearance, but on behavior. People wouldn't treat other people differently because of the color of their skin. And we wouldn't kill 45 billion animals each year for food.
> *Jess, 18, USA*

> Money is power, and it makes people think they can do what they want. People who have a lot of money are more aggressive because they think they can rule the world. They're dangerous because they think that nothing will happen to them if they do something wrong.
> *Pablo, 17, Colombia*

> Love is when two people trust each other completely and always want to be together. It's about taking the good with the bad, and always being ready to say sorr It's the most valuable thing in life.
> *Linda, 16, Ireland*

> My family are my friends—I love all of them. Because I live with my parents they are always with me and if I'm sad, they try to make me feel better. But it's my sister who's the most special person in the world to me. If I ever left home, I'd miss my little sister terribly.
> *Meleike, 15, Sri Lanka*

> I think love means a lot of different things to different people. Some people say love is about family, and others say it is about friends, or ever pets. It's hard to say what it is exactly— it really depends on the person.
> *Shinko, 19, Japan*

> My little sister gives me hope. No matter what's gone wrong during the day, when I come home she always has the same big smile. Then I realize that things can't be too bad.
> *Tina, 17, Australia*

> Global brands like Levi's®, Nike, and Coca-Cola® started becoming really big in my country about ten years ago, and people have gone crazy for them. It's like a sickness, and you see teenagers asking for sneakers that cost twice their parents' monthly salary. I also know people who steal from their parents to buy brand-name goods. They're not stealing for things they really need—it's just that they think they need them.
> *Said, 18, Algeria*

> Money can change your life and help you buy whatever you need. However, it's not the most important thing for me. I know that I need money to buy food so that I can eat. But there are a lot of things money can't buy—love, for example.
> *Markos, 16, Ethiopia*

1 Reading

Read *Happiness and success* and answer the questions.
Who ...

1 knows of teenage thieves? _____
2 is against racism? _____
3 says her mother and father are very important to her? _____
4 thinks love means facing life's ups and downs together? _____
5 has younger sisters? _____
6 thinks money can make people dangerous? _____
7 is probably a vegetarian? _____
8 thinks it's difficult to define love? _____
9 says that love should be about what people do, not what they look like? _____
10 thinks that love is worth more than anything else? _____
11 criticizes the effect of multinational companies? _____
12 says that money can't buy love? _____

2 Reading

Read the text again and match the beginnings with the endings.

1 The girl from Australia ☐
2 Markos realizes that ☐
3 Said thinks that global brands ☐
4 Pablo thinks that having lots of money ☐
5 For the 16-year-old girl, being ready to apologize ☐
6 The oldest person ☐
7 For one of the boys from Africa, other things in life ☐
8 One of the Asian girls thinks of her family ☐
9 The Algerian boy compares teenagers' obsession ☐
10 The youngest girl's parents ☐

a with possessions to a disease.
b are more important than money.
c causes bad behavior.
d try to cheer her up when she is unhappy.
e as the principal thing in her life.
f money is essential for daily living.
g compares different views of love.
h encourage unnecessary consumption.
i is an important part of love.
j loves her sister's smile.

3 Vocabulary

Complete the sentences with these words.

aggressive appearance base behavior brand rule salary trust

1 In the past, the king used to _____ the country.
2 When you're _____, the way you behave shows you want to attack someone.
3 When you _____ someone, you believe that they are good and you can depend on them.
4 If you _____ a decision on something, you use particular facts or ideas to reach your decision.
5 The way someone looks is their _____.
6 A product or group of products made by a particular company is a _____.
7 The money someone earns from a job is their _____.
8 Someone's _____ is the particular way in which they do things.

4 Writing

Write your thoughts on these topics.

Family

Love

Money

2 CREATIVITY

1 I don't think it's art!

Children have been building sandcastles on beaches for hundreds, if not thousands, of years. Their sandcastles are usually simple constructions, made with a bucket and decorated with shells or stones; maybe with a flag on top. However, in places where the sand is particularly good for making sandcastles, sand artists can produce much more complex sculptures.

Since 1986, sand artists have been competing in an annual World Championship of Sand Sculpting. The event started in British Columbia, Canada. The sand on the beaches there sticks together easily when wet, so it is ideal for sculpting. The amazingly beautiful works of art which the competitors produce survive only until the ocean, storms, and wind wash them away.

Because of problems with heavy rain, the competition is now held in the United States, and artists of all ages from all over the world go there to take part.

1 Reading

Read *Sand art*. Then read the sentences and write *T* (true) or *F* (false).

1 Sand artists have been competing in a world championship for over 20 years. ☐

2 The World Championship of Sand Sculpting started in the U.S. ☐

3 Competitors in the World Championship of Sand Sculpting are all children. ☐

4 The competition isn't held in Canada because the ocean washes the sculptures away. ☐

5 The competition moved to the United States because of problems with the weather. ☐

2 Present perfect progressive with *for* and *since*

Write questions and answers.

1 The band started playing at 8 p.m. It's now 8:45 and they're still playing.
   How long has the band been playing?
   They've been playing for *45 minutes.*

2 Jake started painting a picture four hours ago. He's still painting at 3 p.m.
   _____ since _____

3 Sally started learning to drive on May 1. It's now July 1, and she's still learning to drive.
   _____ for _____

4 Robbie turned on the TV 20 minutes ago. It's 9:30 and he's still watching.
   _____ since _____

5 The team started training six weeks ago and they're still training.
   _____ for _____

6 Lizzy called Joe 30 minutes ago. She's still talking to him at 10:15 p.m.
   _____ since _____

7 Paul started making movies in 2001 and he's still making movies.
   _____ for _____

8 The actors are rehearsing a play. They started on Monday and it's now Friday.
   _____ since _____

14

UNIT 2

3 Crossword

Complete the crossword puzzle and find the extra word ↓.

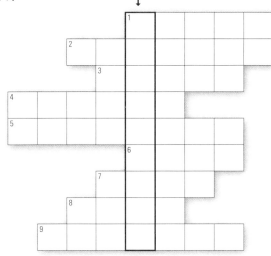

1 Bronze is a kind of …
2 Interior walls are usually covered with … before they are painted.
3 The Great Wall of China is made of …
4 Car tires are made of …
5 Modern parking garages are often made of …
6 Antony Gormley makes many of his sculptures out of …
7 Many beaches consist of …
8 Expensive jewelry is often made of …
9 Goods are often packed in a … substance called Styrofoam™.

4 Vocabulary

Compare the words in list A with the words in list B. Write *S* if they have almost the same meaning, *O* if they are opposites, and *G* if A is more general than B.

	A	B	
1	prize	award	*S*
2	furniture	cupboard	
3	group	gang	
4	appear	disappear	
5	common	unique	
6	art	sculpture	
7	public	private	
8	inside	interior	
9	material	wood	
10	metal	iron	

5 Pronunciation

Write the number of syllables and mark the stress.

■ concrete *2*   cupboard ___   domestic ___

heritage ___   material ___   reappear ___

represent ___   sculpture ___   staircase ___

tribute ___   unique ___   unusual ___

6 Vocabulary

Complete the sentences with these words.

> displayed domestic murder statue
> striking symbol tribute unique

1 The _____ of Liberty in New York is a world-famous structure.
2 Modern kitchens have _____ appliances like dishwashers and freezers.
3 The artist _____ her paintings on the restaurant wall.
4 The bright colors of her paintings make them very _____.
5 The sculpture was created as a _____ to the work of doctors and nurses.
6 People are usually sent to prison for the crime of _____.
7 The _____ @ is used in e-mail addresses.
8 His work is _____—nobody else produces anything like it.

7 Vocabulary

Match the words in list A with the words and phrases in list B. Then write the phrases.

	A	B		
1	cable	example	1	*cable car*
2	waste	house	2	
3	free	still	3	
4	striking	car	4	
5	stand	of charge	5	
6	town	of money	6	

8 Pronunciation

Write these words under *use* or *us*, according to the pronunciation of the underlined letter *u*.

> ~~contin*u*e~~ c*u*lture c*u*pboard h*u*ge h*u*man p*u*blic
> r*u*bber sc*u*lpture stat*u*e st*u*dy trib*u*te *u*nique

/ju/ **use**	/ʌ/ **us**
continue	

> **Extension** Write a short paragraph about your favorite artist or work of art.

2 CREATIVITY
I've been hoping ...

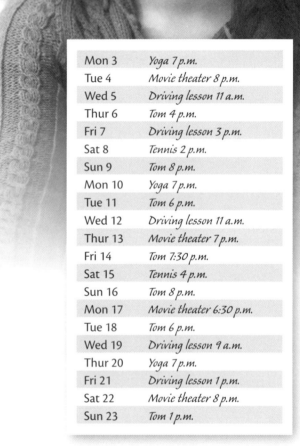

1 Reading

Samantha doesn't have a job right now, but she's been really busy recently. Read her blog and write sentences about what she has and hasn't been doing.

> Guess what? I'm learning to drive! I take lessons on Wednesdays and Fridays, and it's a lot of fun. I also decided last month that I wanted to join a yoga class. There's one at the sports center on Monday evenings. I've now been to my third class and already I feel much better. I'm keeping in shape by playing tennis on Saturdays, too. Sue and Lorna are good at tennis and they are always happy to play a game with me.
>
> The free tickets for the movie theater that I won in that newspaper competition have really been useful. I've been five times this month and I've seen some great movies. Tom likes movies as well, so he's been coming with me. We're looking forward to seeing two or three more movies next week!

Mon 3	Yoga 7 p.m.
Tue 4	Movie theater 8 p.m.
Wed 5	Driving lesson 11 a.m.
Thur 6	Tom 4 p.m.
Fri 7	Driving lesson 3 p.m.
Sat 8	Tennis 2 p.m.
Sun 9	Tom 8 p.m.
Mon 10	Yoga 7 p.m.
Tue 11	Tom 6 p.m.
Wed 12	Driving lesson 11 a.m.
Thur 13	Movie theater 7 p.m.
Fri 14	Tom 7:30 p.m.
Sat 15	Tennis 4 p.m.
Sun 16	Tom 8 p.m.
Mon 17	Movie theater 6:30 p.m.
Tue 18	Tom 6 p.m.
Wed 19	Driving lesson 9 a.m.
Thur 20	Yoga 7 p.m.
Fri 21	Driving lesson 1 p.m.
Sat 22	Movie theater 8 p.m.
Sun 23	Tom 1 p.m.

1 go out with Tom
   She's been going out with Tom.

2 go out with Andy
   She hasn't been going out with Andy.

3 take music lessons

4 take driving lessons

5 do aerobics

6 do yoga

7 play basketball

8 play tennis

9 go to the movies

10 go to the theater

2 Present perfect simple

Look at Samantha's schedule above. It's now the evening of Sunday 23. Write questions and answers about what she has done in the last three weeks.

1 go out with Tom—how often?
   How often has she gone out with Tom?
   Seven times.

2 take driving lessons—how many?

3 see movies—how many?

4 play tennis—how often?

5 do yoga—how often?

UNIT 2

3 Present perfect: simple and progressive

Complete Samantha's e-mail to a friend with the correct form of the verbs.

From: Samantha
To: Kim
Subject: Hi

Sorry I (1) _____ (not be) in touch for so long, but things (2) _____ (be) busy recently. I (3) _____ (try) to find acting work—I (4) _____ (not have) a job for ages. I (5) _____ (make) hundreds of phone calls and I (6) _____ (write) dozens of letters, but no luck so far.

Meanwhile I (7) _____ (learn) to drive, but I (8) _____ (not get) my driver's license yet. And I (9) _____ (look) for an apartment, but I (10) _____ (not find) anything I can afford, so I (11) _____ (stay) with friends for the last couple of months. Hold on—the phone's ringing.

Great news! The agency (12) _____ (just call), and they (13) _____ (offer) me a part in a new TV soap about college students. I'm really glad because I (14) _____ (always want) to work in TV and I (15) _____ (not have) the chance before.

How are you? I hope you (16) _____ (enjoy) your new job. I can't wait to hear about it.

4 Prepositions

Complete with these prepositions.

around   as   for   in   of   on

Plenty (1) _____ young people want to work (2) _____ movies, and it's always fun to see yourself (3) _____ screen. But you have to hang (4) _____ while you're waiting (5) _____ the action, and if you're (6) _____ location, you can get cold and wet. However, if the director catches sight (7) _____ you, who knows?—you could become a star! Hollywood legend Clark Gable started his career (8) _____ an extra in silent movies. He became one (9) _____ the best-known actors (10) _____ the world and won an Academy Award (11) _____ his role in *It Happened One Night*. But few people these days remember stuntman Yakima Canutt, who doubled (12) _____ Gable in *Gone With The Wind*.

5 Vocabulary

The same letters are missing in each line. Complete the words.

1 extraordin_____   necess_____   tempor_____
2 auto_____   para_____   photo_____
3 instruc_____   loca_____   reac_____
4 commerc_____   mater_____   spec_____
5 care_____   help_____   success_____
6 particu_____   regu_____   simi_____

6 Vocabulary

Make a word map for movies.

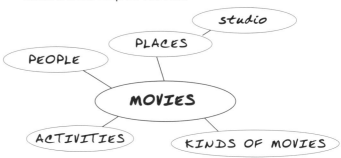

7 Pronunciation

Match the stress patterns with the sentences.

A ■ ▪ ▪ ▪ ■
B ■ ▪ ■ ▪ ■
C ■ ▪ ▪ ■ ■
D ■ ▪ ■ ▪ ▪ ■
E ■ ▪ ▪ ■ ▪ ■ ▪

1 How do you find work?   ☐
2 It does seem quiet.   ☐
3 What's it been like for others? ☐
4 Believe it or not.   ☐
5 How much work have you had?   ☐

Extension If you could be in a movie, as an extra or one of the stars, which movie would it be? Write a paragraph explaining why, describing what you think the experience would be like.

17

CREATIVITY

She had been reading a book

1 Reading

Read the story and complete it with the past perfect simple or progressive form of the verbs.

Spooky story

One winter's night, 16-year-old Daisy was sitting on the couch watching TV. Her parents (1) _____ (go) out to a party. It was cold, and Daisy had a warm blanket around her. It (2) _____ (snow) all afternoon, but the snow (3) _____ (just stop) falling.

Daisy was watching a horror movie, when she suddenly screamed. She (4) _____ (catch) sight of a strange-looking man outside, staring at her through the glass door behind the television set. Terrified, Daisy pulled the blanket over her head, reached for her cell phone, and called the police.

Luckily, the police arrived in a few minutes, and Daisy told them about the strange man she (5) _____ (see) outside the glass door. The police opened the door and went into the yard. After they (6) _____ (look) around, they came back into the house and explained that no one (7) _____ (be) outside because there were no footprints in the snow. Daisy finally agreed that she (8) _____ (imagine) seeing the man because she (9) _____ (watch) a scary movie.

Then one of the police officers looked behind the couch and his face went white. He pointed at wet footprints on the carpet behind the couch. Then Daisy realized that she (10) _____ (not see) the man outside the glass door, she (11) _____ (see) his reflection in the door—because he (12) _____ (stand) behind her!

2 Past perfect simple

Join the sentences using *After* + past perfect simple.

1 The pilot completed the pre-flight checks.
   Then he prepared for take-off.

   After the pilot had completed the pre-flight checks, he prepared for take-off.

2 The ship reached the Bahamas. Then it sailed to Cuba.

3 The climbers took pictures.
   Then they started coming down the mountain.

4 The explorers caught some fish.
   Then they cooked them over a camp fire.

5 We collected some wood. Then we built a shelter.

6 I walked through the forest for three hours.
   Then I found my way out.

7 She saw the movie *Twilight*.
   Then she decided to read the book.

8 He traveled around China.
   Then he wrote a book about the experience.

9 The Coast Guard rescued the children.
   Then they were taken to the hospital.

10 The police arrested the thieves.
   Then they took them to the police station.

UNIT 2

3 Past perfect progressive

Answer the questions using *Because* + the past perfect progressive of these phrases.

> ~~dance all night~~   fight   lie on the beach
> listen to very loud music   steal from stores
> study for a long time   watch a horror movie   work on his car

1 Why was Lucy exhausted?

Because she'd been dancing all night.

2 Why were Tom's hands dirty?

3 Why did the police arrest the woman?

4 Why was Kate scared?

5 Why were the tourists sunburned?

6 Why did Jack have a headache?

7 Why was the teacher angry with the boys?

8 Why weren't the students worried about the exam?

4 Vocabulary

Make eight words by joining pairs below.

~~CHILD~~	TRICITY	AGER	~~HOOD~~
IN	PRE	TION	ICIAL
ABAN	ARTIF	VIOUS	TEEN
SPIRE	DON	ERUP	ELEC

1 *childhood*   **5**
2   **6**
3   **7**
4   **8**

5 Vocabulary

Find words in the text on page 26 of the Student's Book which mean the opposite of these words.

1 tiny
2 started
3 death
4 outdoors
5 beautiful
6 real
7 following

6 Vocabulary

Write the opposites.

1 old person .... person
2 old shoes .... shoes
3 short story .... story
4 short boy .... boy
5 hard task .... task
6 hard bed .... bed
7 right answer .... answer
8 right-hand .... -hand
9 quiet street .... street
10 quiet voice .... voice

7 Vocabulary

Match the words in list A with the words in list B and write six compound nouns.

	A	B		
1	volcanic	war	**1**	*volcanic eruption*
2	horror	eruption	**2**	
3	human	story	**3**	
4	best	show	**4**	
5	world	being	**5**	
6	TV	friend	**6**	

8 Pronunciation

Do they rhyme (✓) or not (✗)?

1 author   rather   ☒
2 dead   need   ☐
3 feel   real   ☐
4 over   cover   ☐
5 friend   send   ☐
6 seem   dream   ☐
7 wrote   poet   ☐
8 war   star   ☐

> **Extension** What was your favorite book when you were a child? Who were the main characters, and which one was your favorite? What was the story about? Write a paragraph about it.

19

2 CREATIVITY

4 Integrated Skills

Telling a folk tale

1 Reading

Read *The Black Tulip* and number paragraphs A–F in the right order.

Now complete the story with these phrases.

a who had also been trying to grow a black tulip

b but the bulb had completely disappeared

c thinking about all the money he was going to win

d and opening into a black flower

e perhaps he could win the prize after all

f but he was sure it would make him rich and famous

g where all the bulbs were kept

h but without any success

i but you ate that for breakfast

The Black Tulip—a Dutch folk tale

A

At last, one of the growers—let's call him Pieter—produced a small bulb which was a mixture of all the darkest colors he had ever grown. He was sure he had produced the first and only black tulip. It was only a small bulb, but he could imagine it growing (**1**) .... He didn't even think of the prize money. He knew the black tulip would be the most valuable flower in the world, but for him it would be the most beautiful.

B

The following day, his housekeeper found what looked like an onion on the shelf. "Odd place for an onion," she thought. "Oh, well, it will make a nice omelet." So she took the "onion" into the kitchen. She chopped it up, added two eggs, and gave her master an onion omelet for breakfast. The thief ate the omelet happily, (**2**) ....

C

That night, he left his house and went to Pieter's backyard. He went through the gate and up to the great glass greenhouse (**3**) .... It was dark, so he struck a match and quickly moved along the lines of bulbs. Each bulb was labeled and finally he found what he had been looking for—a bulb labeled "The Black Tulip." After he had put the bulb in his pocket and placed another bulb where the black tulip bulb had been, he hurried home. Back inside his house, the thief put the bulb carefully on a shelf in the dining room. It looked like any other tulip bulb, (**4**) ....

D

Many years ago, there was a competition in Holland. A prize of one thousand gold crowns was offered to the first person who could grow a black tulip. People had been trying to grow a black tulip for years, (**5**) .... Now there was great activity among the tulip growers. They tried everything they could to grow a black tulip.

E

As soon as he had finished his breakfast, he went over to the shelf. Where had the bulb gone?! In a panic he looked everywhere, (**6**) .... He asked all his servants—no, they hadn't seen a tulip bulb. Then he asked if they had seen anything unusual. "Only an old onion," said his housekeeper, "(**7**) ...." Suddenly the thief began to feel sick. He went to bed and decided never to steal again. And the world is still waiting for the first black tulip.

F

Pieter tried to keep the news of his bulb a secret. The only people he told were his family and closest friends. But the secret reached the ears of another bulb grower, (**8**) .... This man wanted to win the prize of a thousand gold crowns. Now Pieter had beaten him to it—or had he? The man started to make a plan— (**9**) ....

2 Writing

Answer the questions.

1 Why did Pieter believe he had produced the first black tulip bulb?

2 Why didn't he think about the prize money?

3 Why did he want to keep the news of his bulb a secret?

4 Why did the thief steal the black tulip bulb?

5 Why did the housekeeper cook the bulb?

6 What did the thief ask all his servants first?

7 Why did the thief begin to feel sick?

8 When do you think Pieter discovered the theft of the black tulip?

9 How do you think he felt?

10 What do you think he did?

3 Crossword

Complete the crossword puzzle.

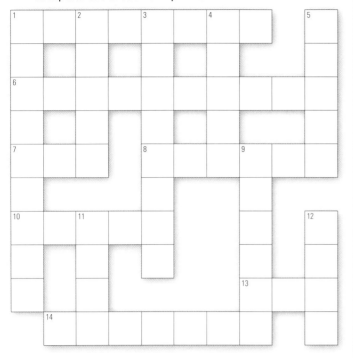

Across →

1. Opposite of *guilty*. (8)
6. Exciting, and sometimes dangerous, experiences. (10)
7. Another word for *sick*. (3)
8. The professor couldn't swim and, as a ..., he drowned. (6)
10. Mary Shelley had been reading a book ... chemistry. (5)
13. Many artists ... natural materials in their work. (3)
14. Chris Ofili painted *No Woman No Cry* as a ... to the Lawrence family. (7)

Down ↓

1. The people in the story aren't real—they're ... (9)
2. Lots of people dream of writing a successful ... (5)
3. Rachel Whiteread's sculpture *House* was made of ... (8)
4. The words *treatment* and *amazement* are ... formed from verbs. (5)
5. Where filming takes place in a studio. (2, 3)
9. There's nothing else like it—it's ... (6)
11. The ferryman had taken ... the job from his father. (4)
12. He'd started the job when he was 16 and had been doing it ... since. (4)

LEARNER INDEPENDENCE

Telling a story

When telling stories, we use various narrative words and structures to show the sequence of events.

Which of these can you find in *The Black Tulip*?

- Time adverbs and phrases:
  then, soon, suddenly, afterwards, in the end, finally, eventually, at last, later
  Many years ago ... That night ... The next/following day ...
- Clauses beginning with:
  after, as soon as, before, until, when, while
- Narrative tenses, in particular:
  simple past and past progressive
  past perfect simple and past perfect progressive

When you read stories, notice the narrative words and structures. Try to use them when you are writing stories.

Extensive reading

Read an English book and imagine you are a movie director making a movie of the story. Which actors will you choose to play the main characters in your movie, and why?

2 CREATIVITY

Inspired EXTRA!

CONSOLIDATION

LESSON 1

Write questions beginning *How long ...?* with the present perfect progressive and answer them using both *for* and *since*. For answers with *since*, use the present time as a reference point.

1 Jamie started playing the guitar last month.

How long has Jamie been playing the guitar?

For a month. Since ...

2 Susie started painting her room two days ago.

3 Rob started cooking dinner half an hour ago.

4 Dave started learning Spanish six months ago.

5 Holly and Ben started traveling around the world four weeks ago.

LESSON 2

Write sentences using the present perfect simple and the present perfect progressive with the phrases in *italics*.

1 Sarah/take pictures   *30 minutes   60 pictures*

Sarah has been taking pictures for 30 minutes.

She's taken 60 pictures.

2 Rick/write e-mails   *15 minutes   3 e-mails*

3 Kate/apply for jobs   *6 months   9 jobs*

4 Maria and Paul/drive   *5 hours   450 kilometers*

5 Pete and Helen/record songs   *2 weeks   20 songs*

LESSON 3

Write sentences using the past perfect progressive.

What had the people been doing before the electricity went out?

1 Alex/cook supper

Alex had been cooking dinner.

2 Dan/watch TV

3 Alice/play computer games

4 Mike/listen to music

5 Tammy/dry her hair

6 Sam/download songs

LESSON 4

Write questions for these answers about *The Professor and the Wise Ferryman*.

1 Where   *did the ferryman live?*
In a hut by the Ganges River in India.

2 How much
Hardly enough to feed his family.

3 How
By listening to his passengers.

4 What
A nice suit and well-polished shoes.

5 Why
Because he'd never been to school.

6 Why
Because he hadn't learned to swim.

Spelling

Fill in the silent letters of these words from Unit 2.

1 b___ilding   **2** cu___board   **3** c___emistry   **4** extr___ordinary

5 fo___k   **6** ___nowle___ge   **7** ___nown   **8** li___tning

9 mi___t   **10** s___ene   **11** uniq___e

Brainteaser

Which English word is always pronounced incorrectly?

Answer on page 25.

22

UNIT 2

EXTENSION

LESSON 1

Write eight sentences—about yourself, your family, or your friends—using the present perfect progressive of these verbs + *for* or *since*.

> feel   have   hope   live   look   sit   try   use

LESSON 2

Correct the sentences.

1 Jon has been looking for work ~~since~~ *for* six months.
2 Dan has been having two jobs this year.
3 How long have you read *Frankenstein*?
4 How many text messages have you been sending today?
5 They've been watching TV for six o'clock.
6 I've been seeing six movies this month.
7 How many TV have you watched recently?
8 How long did you know your best friend?

LESSON 3

Complete the sentences using the past perfect progressive—and your imagination.

1 Dan had a red face because
2 Meg had tears in her eyes because
3 Bert had a black eye because
4 Sara was fed up because
5 The students were tired because
6 The children were cold because

LESSON 4

Think about a wise person that you know. Write a paragraph explaining why you think this person is wise.

Web watch

MOMA, the Museum of Modern Art, is an art museum in New York City. Find the official website on the Internet. Select "Explore" and click on "The Collection" to see its collections and displays. Find an interesting or unusual work of art and describe it to your partner.

Spelling

Complete the words with *-ance* or *-ence*.

1 ambul........   2 appear........   3 bal........
4 differ........   5 dist........   6 evid........
7 import........   8 independ........   9 influ........
10 perform........   11 sci........   12 sent........
13 sequ........   14 sil........

Brainteaser

Five pieces of coal, a carrot, and a scarf were lying on the ground. No one had put them on the ground—so how did they get there?

Answer on page 25.

REVIEW
UNITS 1–2

1 Read the text. For each number 1–15, choose word or phrase A, B, C, or D.

The man, the boy, and the donkey

Many years ago, a man and his son were walking with their donkey to a market. The market town was several miles from their village, so they (**1**) _____ their journey early that morning.

After they (**2**) _____ beside the donkey for a little while, they passed a young man who said, "You stupid people, a donkey is (**3**) _____ riding on! Why aren't you riding it?"

So the man put the boy on the donkey and they went on their way. After they (**4**) _____ another mile, they met a group of men, one of whom said, "Look at that lazy boy on the donkey—and his poor old father (**5**) _____ really tired!"

As soon as the son heard this, he (**6**) _____ down, and his father got on the donkey. But they (**7**) _____ far when they passed two women, one of whom said to the other, "Look at that lazy man on the donkey—and his poor little son (**8**) _____ exhausted because he (**9**) _____ for such a long time!"

The man didn't know what to do, but eventually he lifted his son up onto the donkey as well. By this time they (**10**) _____ the town, and people started pointing and laughing at them. "How can you treat your donkey like that?" they cried. "It will collapse under the weight of you both!"

Then the man and boy both got off the donkey and tried (**11**) _____ what to do. After (**12**) _____ for a while, they cut down a pole, tied the donkey's feet to it, and raised the pole and the donkey onto their shoulders. They walked on (**13**) _____ a few minutes until they came to a bridge over a river. Suddenly the donkey started to struggle, and the boy couldn't help (**14**) _____ his end of the pole. As a result, the donkey fell into the river and drowned.

"That will teach you," said a wise old man who (**15**) _____ them. "Try to please everyone, and you will please no one."

1	A started	B have started	C had started	D had been starting
2	A walking	B walked	C have been walking	D had been walking
3	A by	B for	C to	D after
4	A walking	B walked	C had walked	D had been walking
5	A becomes	B became	C has become	D had become
6	A jumped	B has jumped	C has been jumping	D had jumped
7	A went	B didn't go	C had gone	D hadn't gone
8	A seems	B is seeming	C has seemed	D has been seeming
9	A walks	B is walking	C walked	D has been walking
10	A reached	B have reached	C had reached	D had been reaching
11	A decide	B to decide	C deciding	D by deciding
12	A think	B thinking	C they have thought	D they have been thinking
13	A for	B since	C after	D during
14	A drop	B to drop	C dropping	D he dropped
15	A followed	B has followed	C has been following	D had been following

2 Complete with the correct form of the words in capitals.

1. We lived by the ocean during our _____.   CHILD
2. We all stared at the sculpture in _____.   AMAZE
3. *Frankenstein* is a story about the _____ of artificial life.   CREATE
4. Add the tomatoes and stir the _____ over a low heat.   MIX
5. She's a _____ person and she doesn't take risks.   SENSE
6. The _____ on the player's knee was successful.   OPERATE
7. It's _____ to eat too much junk food.   HEALTH
8. A little _____ is a dangerous thing!   KNOW

24

3 Complete the second sentence so that it means the same as the first sentence.

1 She read the book after seeing the movie.
Before _____

2 You can use this gadget to open bottles.
You can use this gadget for _____

3 You press a button to start the machine.
You start the machine by _____

4 It isn't hard to create a website.
Creating _____

5 You met him last year—do you remember?
Do you remember _____ ?

6 Please lock the door when you leave the house.
Don't forget _____

7 After doing his homework, he went out.
When he _____

8 It started raining a few minutes ago.
_____ for a few minutes.

4 Find the word that is different.

1 boil   fry   roast   stir
2 beat   chop   cut   slice
3 bronze   gold   iron   metal
4 dangerous   harmful   healthy   risky
5 fact   myth   reality   truth
6 brain   collar   heart   muscle
7 hurry   run   rush   walk
8 damage   hurt   improve   injure
9 exactly   frequently   regularly   usually

Answers to Brainteasers

UNIT 1
Consolidation Nothing.
Extension The surgeon was the boy's mother.

UNIT 2
Consolidation "Incorrectly".
Extension They had been on a snowman before the snow melted. (coal for eyes and buttons, a carrot for the nose)

LEARNER INDEPENDENCE
SELF ASSESSMENT

Vocabulary

1 Draw this chart in your notebook. How many words can you write in each category?

More than 10? Good!   *More than 12?* Very good!
More than 15? Excellent!

Food and drink	
Health and illness	
Materials	

2 Put the words in order to make expressions from the phrasebooks in Lesson 4 in Units 1 and 2.

1 wrong that with what's
   What's wrong with that?

2 not to idea good it's a …

3 hand other the on

4 thing is sensible the to …

5 waste a it's of money complete

6 or believe not it

7 no for there's excuse …

8 might well as you …

Check your answers.
8/8 Excellent!   *6/8* Very good!   *4/8* Try again!

My learning diary
In Units 1 and 2:
My favorite topic is _____

My favorite picture is _____

The three lessons I like most are _____

My favorite activity or exercise is _____

Something I don't understand is _____

Something I want to learn more about is _____

25

3 SCIENCE AND DISCOVERY

1 Light travels incredibly fast

1 Reading

Read and complete the text with these words.

accurately   approximately   better   extremely   far   farther   slowly   usually

How many planets are there?

Astronomers—scientists who study space—have decided that there are only eight, and not nine, planets going around the Sun. In 2003, a rocky object which was bigger than Pluto was discovered. It was named 2003 UB313, but is more (1) _____ known by its nickname Xena. This discovery made astronomers realize that they had to describe planets more (2) _____. Their new definition means that Pluto is no longer a planet. Along with Xena and an object called Ceres, which is between Mars and Jupiter, Pluto is now described as a "dwarf planet." These dwarf planets go around the Sun more (3) _____ than the other planets, taking more than 200 years to complete the orbit.

And more dwarf planets will be discovered in the future. Plans to build an ELT (4) (_____ Large Telescope) mean that scientists will soon be able to look (5) _____ into space than ever before. Right now, astronomers can see (6) _____ into the universe with a VLT (Very Large Telescope), but the ELT will be able to pick out small objects even (7) _____. Astronomers dream of building a 100-meter-wide telescope called an OWL (Overwhelmingly Large Telescope), but its structure would need the same amount of steel as the Eiffel Tower, and it would cost (8) _____ two billion dollars.

2 Comparison of adverbs

Complete the sentences using information from the chart and these adverbs: *far, quickly, slowly*.

Planets	Distance from Sun (millions of kms)	Time to rotate	Time to go around Sun
Mercury	58	59 days	88 days
Earth	150	1 day	1 year
Jupiter	778	9 hours 50 minutes	11 years 315 days
Neptune	4,498	16 hours 7 minutes	164 years 321 days

1 Light has to travel __*farther*__ from the Sun to Earth than to Mercury.
2 Jupiter rotates _____ of the four planets.
3 Earth goes around the Sun _____ than Jupiter.
4 Mercury rotates _____ than Neptune.
5 A spacecraft would have to travel much _____ from Earth to get to Neptune than to Jupiter.
6 Mercury goes around the Sun _____ of the four planets.
7 Neptune rotates _____ than Earth.
8 Neptune goes around the Sun _____ of the four planets.
9 Light has to travel _____ from the Sun to Neptune.
10 Jupiter goes around the Sun _____ than Mercury.

26

UNIT 3

3 Comparison of adverbs

Complete with the correct form of these adverbs.
You can use them more than once.

> badly far fast hard often slowly well

1 The wise man said, "Do what works ___*best*___
   for you—don't listen to other people."

2 We lost the game—the whole team played
   _____ than usual, but the goalkeeper
   played _____ of all.

3 The early astronauts had to work _____
   than more recent ones.

4 The competition to see who could run
   _____ in 24 hours was won by Lucy,
   who ran 15 kilometers _____ than last
   year's winner.

5 I feel bad. I'm not getting _____—I feel
   _____ today than yesterday.

6 Most people think _____ than they can
   type, or in other words, they type _____
   than they think.

7 People should complain about bad food in restaurants
   _____ than they do.

4 Position and order of adverbial phrases

Put the adverbial phrases in the right order.

1 Sergei Avdeyev flew _____.
   (for 747 days/in space)

2 Valeri Polyakov stayed up _____.
   (the longest/in a spacecraft)

3 Space flight developed _____.
   (in the 1960s/quickly)

4 Neil Armstrong walked _____.
   (in July 1969/on the Moon)

5 Astronauts appear to walk _____
   _____.
   (on the Moon/strangely)

6 A Russian and an American both walked
   _____.
   (in space/in 1965)

7 Conrad and Bean walked _____
   _____.
   (in 1969/successfully/on the Moon)

5 Vocabulary

Match the verbs in list A with the words and phrases in
list B. Then write the phrases.

	A	B		
1	breathe	a ton	1	*breathe oxygen*
2	disagree	in size	2	_____
3	expand	distance	3	_____
4	measure	about something	4	_____
5	weigh	oxygen	5	_____

6 Vocabulary

Find words on pages 36–37 of the Student's Book
which mean the opposite of these words.

1 closest _____

2 destroyed _____

3 getting smaller _____

4 exactly _____

5 not surprising _____

6 slowly _____

7 Vocabulary

Complete the sentences.

1 4,500,000,000 is ___*four and a half billion.*___

2 2,000,000,000,000 is _____

3 3,575,000 is _____

4 6,400,000,000,000 is _____

5 625,000 is _____

8 Pronunciation

Write the number of syllables and mark the stress.

■

accurately _4_   approximately ___   astonishing ___

equator ___   expand ___   organism ___   oxygen ___

percentage ___   rotate ___   universe ___

> **Extension** Use the chart in exercise 2 to
> write three more fill-in-the-blank sentences for
> other students to complete.

3.2 SCIENCE AND DISCOVERY
What a fantastic sight!

1 Reading
Read the text and answer the questions.

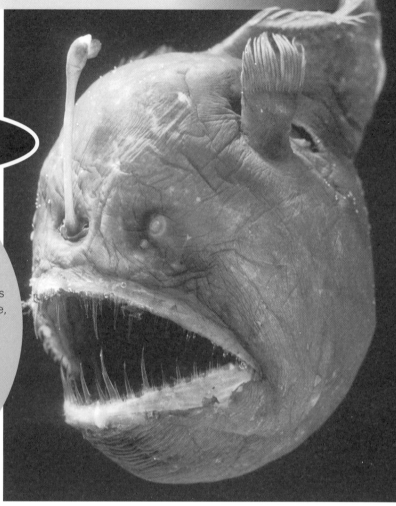

Anglerfish

There are more than 200 species of anglerfish. They are usually dark gray in color and they have huge heads and enormous mouths filled with sharp teeth. Some can be really large, reaching up to a meter in length. They live in the depths of the ocean, up to a mile below the surface. Down there it is so dark that it is difficult to see anything. It is, therefore, difficult for the creatures that live there to find food.

The anglerfish has developed a "fishing rod," actually part of its spine, which sticks out over the top of its head near its mouth. The tip of this rod gives off light. Light at this depth is such an unusual sight that other fish swim up to it to see what it is. The anglerfish then catches and eats them. Its mouth is so big that it can swallow fish up to twice its own size.

1 Why is it difficult to see anything a mile below the surface of the ocean?

2 What problem do fish that live very deep in the ocean have?

3 How has the anglerfish solved this problem?

4 Why do other fish swim up to the anglerfish?

5 Why can the anglerfish swallow fish which are much bigger than itself?

2 What (a/an) ...! so/such (a/an) ...

Complete with *What (a/an)* or *so/such (a/an)*.

PETRA HARDY (1) *What an* ugly fish!

PILOT It's an anglerfish. Look at the "fishing rod" on its head.

PETRA HARDY Wow! Why does it have that?

PILOT It's (2) .... dark down here that it is difficult to see anything. The anglerfish uses the light on its rod to catch other fish.

PETRA HARDY (3) .... smart idea! And look at its mouth. (4) .... lot of teeth!

PILOT Yes, and it has (5) .... big mouth that it can swallow fish much bigger than itself.

PETRA HARDY (6) .... amazing sight!

UNIT 3

3 Result clauses: *so/such ... that*

Join the sentences using *so/such ... that*.

1 The water was cold. No one went swimming.

The water was so cold that no one went swimming.

2 Amy was a good guitar player. They didn't want her to stop.

3 The fish was delicious. Paul asked for some more.

4 It was a beautiful rainbow. Sam took a picture of it.

5 It was a huge crab. Sue screamed.

6 It was a great party. No one wanted to leave.

4 Order of adjectives

Complete the chart with these adjectives.

adult American ancient big colorless
delicious international large Mexican modern
multicolored pink pretty Russian short
smart tall teenage unexpected yellow

Opinion	Size	Age	Shape	Color	Origin

5 Order of adjectives

Put the adjectives in the right order.

1 Julie was playing a
_____ guitar. (American, fantastic, new)

2 Jim was wearing a
_____ jacket. (blue, comfortable, long, old)

3 We all saw a
_____ rainbow. (brightly-colored, fantastic, big)

4 Ann was wearing a
_____ skirt. (Italian, beautiful, new, short)

5 Jeff was cooking
_____ shrimp. (delicious, fresh, large, pink)

6 It was a
_____ crab. (frightening, giant, green, round)

6 Vocabulary

Compare the words in list A with the words in list B. Write *S* if they have almost the same meaning, *O* if they are opposites, and *G* if A is more general than B.

	A	B	
1	bottom	top	*O*
2	species	shrimp	
3	unexpected	surprising	
4	computer	laptop	
5	average	typical	
6	depth	height	
7	remove	take away	
8	look	peer	
9	salty	sweet	
10	descend	go down	

7 Pronunciation

Write the number of syllables and mark the stress.

■
chimney *2*   descend _____   disturb _____

evaporate _____   observer _____   rainbow _____

spacious _____   submersible _____   underwater _____

unexpected _____   volcano _____

8 Pronunciation

Do they rhyme (✓) or not (✗)?

1	blog	flag	✗
2	meter	liter	☐
3	mystery	history	☐
4	mussel	muscle	☐
5	peer	clear	☐
6	push	brush	☐
7	through	though	☐
8	tiny	shiny	☐

Extension Write a short conversation between Petra Hardy and one of the people in the submersible. Try to use expressions such as *What a/an ...!* and *so/such a/an*, and adjectives to describe what they see.

29

3 SCIENCE AND DISCOVERY

3 It won't be cheap

1 Reading

Read and complete the text with these words.

afford air believe colony dream flights
hotel human risk robots spaceships
species temperature tourism will won't

Space (1) _____ promises a new kind of adventure vacation—visit a space station, check into a space (2) _____, and even do a space walk! When space (3) _____ become cheaper, "ordinary" people will be able to (4) _____ them. But how many people will want to (5) _____ their lives when there is a chance of not coming back? Still, it's early days, and (6) _____ will definitely become safer.

Meanwhile, the European Space Agency has started a new project which it hopes will lead to the first (7) _____ flight to Mars. Its ExoMars project will send (8) _____ to explore the Red Planet to search for resources, and even life. But it will be a long time before there is a (9) _____ on Mars, or even on the Moon. And it (10) _____ be easy to live in these places. On the Moon, the (11) _____ rises to more than 100°C and falls to less than −100°C, and it's not much better on Mars.

However, (12) _____ it or not, experts say that one day humans (13) _____ definitely live on other planets. It may sound unlikely, but let's not forget that (14) _____ travel once seemed to be an impossible (15) _____. And some people even believe that we will have to leave Earth for the survival of our (16) _____.

2 Talking about the future

Complete with the most suitable form of the verbs: simple future, simple present, or present progressive.

It's 2050 …

MAX Where (1) _____ you _____ (go) for your vacation this year?

ZARA I (2) _____ (spend) a week in the Cosmo space hotel.

MAX Oh, that (3) _____ (be) fun! (4) _____ you _____ (travel) with friends?

ZARA Yes, I (5) _____ (go) with two friends from work. Our spaceship (6) _____ (take) off on August 15.

MAX What time (7) _____ your flight _____ (depart)?

ZARA At 7:25 a.m., and it (8) _____ (arrive) at the space hotel at 9:15 a.m.

MAX Exciting! I'm sure you (9) _____ (have) a great time.

ZARA I hope so. On the last day of our vacation, I (10) _____ (do) a space walk.

MAX Really? (11) _____ you _____ (not be) scared?

ZARA No, I think it (12) _____ (be) less scary than skydiving! And what (13) _____ you _____ (do) this summer?

MAX I (14) _____ (take) a trip to Mars.

ZARA Wow—you (15) _____ (be) away for a very long time!

30

UNIT 3

3 Talking about the future

Complete with 'll/will, won't, or (be) going to.

TOM What (1) .... (you/sing) now?

AMY I (2) .... (not sing) anything—
I (3) .... (have) something to eat.

TOM Good idea. I (4) .... (bring) you a plate of shrimp.

AMY Mmm, delicious. (5) .... (you/get) me some salad, too?

TOM Sure. Hey, what's Paul doing?

AMY He (6) .... (rescue) his hat. It blew out to sea.

TOM But I'm sure he (7) .... (not reach) it—look, it's moving further away.

AMY I hope he (8) .... (swim) too far.

TOM Paul, come back! We (9) .... (buy) you another hat!

4 Vocabulary

Complete the sentences with the correct form of these verbs.

| come count hold look put take |

1 I'll come shopping with you— .... on a minute while I get my wallet.

2 You can .... down over the city from the top of the tower.

3 I'd like to join the tour—could you .... my name down?

4 Do you think the cost of air travel will go up or .... down?

5 We .... off at 10:25, so we should get to the airport by around 8:30.

6 The rocket is due to take off and we're going to .... down from ten to zero.

5 Vocabulary

Match these words and phrases with their definitions.

| aluminum deposit elevator
honeymoon orbit v rumor |

1 a first payment for something expensive
....

2 information which may not be true
....

3 vacation after a wedding
....

4 move around an object in space
....

5 a lightweight, silver metal
....

6 a machine that carries people up and down
....

6 Vocabulary

The same letters are missing in each line. Complete the words.

1 fact............   hist............   mem............
2 elev............   simul............   calcul............
3 weightless............   busi............   ill............
4 expens............   alternat............   posit............
5 luxur............   spac............   delic............
6 vaca............   popula............   produc............

7 Vocabulary

Write compound nouns beginning with *space* from pages 40–41 of the Student's Book. Notice whether the compound nouns are one word or two words.

....
....
....

8 Pronunciation

Write the number of syllables and mark the stress.

astronaut _3_   elevator ....   experience ....

grandchildren ....   honeymoon ....   luxurious ....

production ....   rumor ....   simulator ....

Extension Imagine you are spending your vacation on the Moon. Send an e-mail home.

31

3 SCIENCE AND DISCOVERY

4 Integrated Skills

Describing events and consequences

1 Reading

Read *More people who Changed the World* and match paragraphs 1–4 with the pictures A–D.

Then complete the text with eight of the phrases a–j. There are two extra phrases.

a about our universe
b until many years after his death
c so no one believed it
d to reach higher floors
e in stores and supermarkets
f because it was extremely popular
g for stopping an elevator in an emergency
h it was the first man-made orbiting satellite
i which was later developed into a commercial freezer
j that the Earth orbited the Sun

More people who Changed the World

1 Picture ....

Have you ever stood in an elevator and wondered if it might crash to the ground? There's no need to worry! In 1854, the American engineer Elisha Graves Otis invented a safety brake (**1**) .... Three years later, he designed the first passenger elevators in the United States. Thanks to Otis, people no longer had to climb hundreds of stairs (**2**) .... , and consequently buildings could be much taller. Without Otis there probably wouldn't be any skyscrapers!

2 Picture ....

The telescope was invented in Holland in 1608. The Italian astronomer Galileo Galilei heard about this new invention in 1609, and so he immediately built his own telescope. He used it to prove his controversial theory (**3**) .... He also used it to make important discoveries about the Moon, the planets, and the stars. Thanks to Galileo, we now know much more (**4**) ....

3 Picture ....

In 1925, the American inventor Clarence Birdseye created the world's first quick-frozen food. He managed to develop a freezing process which not only preserved food safely, but also preserved its taste and appearance. He then invented a fast-freezing machine (**5**) .... As a result of his work, there is now a huge variety of frozen food available (**6**) ....

4 Picture ....

Our world of modern global communications began on October 4, 1957, when the former Soviet Union sent Sputnik 1 into space—(**7**) .... It was created by aircraft engineer and rocket designer Sergei Pavlovich Korolyov, but because of the Cold War, his achievement wasn't publicly recognized (**8**) .... Also thanks to Korolyov, Yuri Gagarin made the first manned space flight in 1961.

2 Writing

Complete these sentences using information from the text.

1 Elisha Graves Otis invented a safety brake which

2 Buildings could be much taller because

3 Galileo Galilei built a telescope after

4 We know much more about our universe as a result of

5 Thanks to Clarence Birdseye, frozen food

6 The Soviet Union sent Sputnik 1 into space, and consequently

32

3 Crossword

Complete the crossword puzzle.

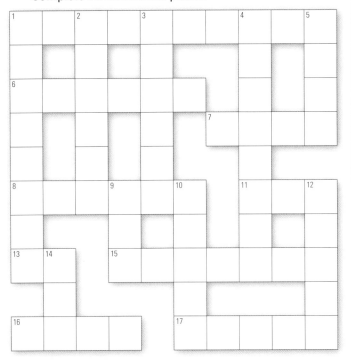

Across →
1. Submersibles are designed to go ... (10)
6. Pasteur's work had a major ... on medical treatment. (6)
7. The Earth orbits the Sun ... every 365.25 days. (4)
8. The Earth doesn't ... at all at the poles. (6)
11. You can see lines of longitude and latitude on a ... (3)
13. Short for *for example*. (2)
15. Imaginary circle around the Earth exactly halfway between the poles. (7)
16. Sailors used to figure out their latitude by looking at the ...s. (4)
17. The plane takes off at 10 a.m. and ... at 11:30 a.m. (5)

Down ↓
1. The Big Bang created our ... (8)
2. Opposite of *arrive*. (6)
3. Something that happened a short time ago is a ... event. (6)
4. Marconi managed to ... radio signals across the Atlantic Ocean. (8)
5. You can ... a spaceship simulator at the Astronaut Hall of Fame. (4)
9. Adjectives such as *young*, *modern*, and *old* all describe ... (3)
10. One light year is ... to 9.5 trillion kilometers! (5)
12. Legs, arms, and hands are all ... of the body. (5)
14. *expand* = ... bigger (3)

LEARNER INDEPENDENCE

Expanding vocabulary

You can use a variety of adjectives to describe things and express your opinion of them. Add as many adjectives as you can to this word map.

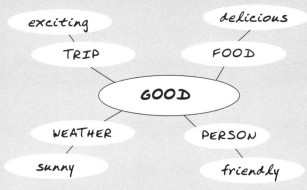

Now make a similar word map for BAD using the same four topics.

Extensive reading

Read an English book and choose two of the main characters. Write a paragraph saying what you think they will do after the end of the story.

3 SCIENCE AND DISCOVERY
Inspired EXTRA!

CONSOLIDATION

LESSON 1

Complete with the comparative and superlative forms of the adverbs.

Adverb	Comparative	Superlative
accurately	*more accurately*	*most accurately*
badly		
early		
far		
fast		
late		
long		
quickly		
slowly		
well		

LESSON 2

Complete with *What (a/an)* or *so/such (a/an)*.

1 *What an* unexpected sight!
2 The ocean floor in the Azores is at _____ great depth that no sunlight reaches it.
3 The water coming from the vents is _____ hot.
4 The Rainbow Vents are _____ beautiful sight.
5 _____ amazing creatures!
6 Going down in the submersible was _____ exciting.
7 It was lucky that Petra had _____ good weather for her dive.
8 Removing the salt from sea water takes _____ long time!

LESSON 3

Complete with the most suitable form of the verbs: simple future, simple present, or present progressive.

Tina (**1**) *is seeing* (see) her best friend Ann on Saturday. It (**2**) _____ (be) the last time that Tina and Ann meet this year. That's because Ann (**3**) _____ (move) to Florida soon. Tina knows that she (**4**) _____ (be) sad when Ann is gone. Unfortunately Ann's flight (**5**) _____ (leave) early in the morning.
So Tina (**6**) _____ (not be) able to go to the airport. But she (**7**) _____ (go) to Florida to see Ann in January. It (**8**) _____ (be) great for the two friends to be together again.

LESSON 4

Complete the questions for these answers about *People who Changed the World* on page 42 of the Student's Book.

1 What *did Pasteur discover?*
   That there were germs called *bacteria* in the air.
2 What _____
   Pasteur's pioneering work.
3 What _____
   A massive protest against environmental pollution.
4 When _____
   On December 12, 1901.
5 Where _____
   In Newfoundland.

Spelling

Correct the spelling of these words from Unit 3 by doubling one letter in each word.

1 acurate 2 aproximate 3 botom 4 depest 5 dolar
6 musel 7 narow 8 pasenger 9 proces 10 sucessfully
11 trilion 12 transmision 13 vacination 14 weightlesness

Brainteaser

What is always coming but never arrives?

Answer on page 49.

34

UNIT 3

EXTENSION

LESSON 1

Look at *What on Earth?* on page 36 of the Student's Book. Complete these questions about the text and answer them.

1 When _____
_____ ?

2 How big _____
_____ ?

3 How fast _____
_____ ?

4 How old _____
_____ ?

5 How much _____
_____ ?

6 How far _____
_____ ?

7 Where _____
_____ ?

8 What _____
_____ ?

LESSON 2

Complete using *so/such* and your own ideas.

1 The movie was _____ funny that she
_____

2 It was _____ a boring book that I
_____

3 It was _____ a great CD that he
_____

4 The restaurant was _____ good that they
_____

5 She was _____ a nice person that we
_____

6 He was _____ angry that he didn't
_____

7 They were _____ late that they
_____

8 I had _____ a wonderful birthday that I
_____

LESSON 3

Complete these sentences for yourself using the most suitable form of the verbs: simple future, simple present, or present progressive.

1 My next English class is on _____
(*day of the week*) and it _____ (begin) at
_____ (*time*).

2 Tonight I _____ (go) to bed at
_____ (*time*).

3 I hope that one day I _____ (be) able to
_____ (*activity*).

4 Tomorrow morning I _____ (get up) at
_____ (*time*) and _____ (have)
breakfast at _____ (*time*).

5 My next school day is on _____
(*day of the week*) and school _____ (start)
at _____ (*time*).

6 _____ I ever _____ (visit)
_____ (*place*)? I don't know.

LESSON 4

Look at exercise 6 on page 43 of the Student's Book and think about the discussion you had. Write a paragraph giving your opinion and that of two other students.

Web watch

Chindogu is a Japanese term for inventions that are practical but also useless. Type *"chindogu"* into *images.google.com* to find pictures of these inventions. Choose one and print it out. Find out what it does and try to "sell" the invention to the other students in your class.

Spelling

Read and complete these words from Unit 3.

The sound /əl/ at the end of a word can be written *-al, -ul,* and *-le.*

1 beautif_____   2 chemic_____   3 comfortab_____

4 controversi_____   5 environment_____   6 impossib_____

7 incredib_____   8 loc_____   9 medic_____   10 natur_____

11 sign_____   12 submersib_____

Brainteaser

What was born at the same time as the Earth, will last as long as the Earth, but is never more than five weeks old?

Answer on page 49.

35

3 Culture

Teenagers who make a difference

Two years ago, teenager Stacey Dooley was working at the perfume counter at an airport. Then she took part in a TV series called *Blood, Sweat, and T-shirts* in which a group of fashion-conscious young people were sent to work in India's "sweatshop" clothes industry.

Stacey was deeply affected by what she saw during this experience, particularly the poverty all around her, and the conditions in the clothes factories where young people of her own age were working. These workers were paid very little for their work, but the clothes they made were sold abroad for large amounts of money. The show made her see how fortunate she and her friends back home were. When the TV series finished, she came back home and gave up her job. She now works as a campaigner, trying to help people all over the world who are not as well off as she is.

James Peterson, a 17-year-old student, has launched a campaign against bullying. Some teenagers from his school stopped his little brother Don in the street and stole his cell phone and his new sneakers. James has designed and produced a range of baseball caps with anti-bullying messages.

He hopes that teenagers will buy these to demonstrate their opposition to bullying in schools and to show that they have decided not to be bullies themselves. As well as selling his baseball caps to students at his own school and other schools in his area, James talks to teachers and police officers who deal with teenagers who are involved in bullying and street crime. He hopes that they will help him with the campaign. He has also persuaded people in the music industry to help promote his campaign by wearing his baseball caps.

His brother was very upset by his experience of bullying and this had an enormous effect on James and gave him the inspiration for this campaign.

A teenager's dream of improving his neighborhood by running free dance classes for young people has come true after he won a national contest. Wacky Rymel, 16, came first in the contest, which was organized with the aim of finding a young person with an inspiring plan to improve their local community.

Wacky will now receive money to hold free street dance classes for other teenagers in his neighborhood for six months. He will also get audio equipment, a place to hold the classes, and costumes for his students. At the end of the six months, he will be given details of ways to get more funding so he can carry on his dance classes.

Wacky, who has just started college, said: "I'm very, very pleased to win this; it was a really tough contest, with many entries, so I'm really happy I've gotten this opportunity to get my idea going. I've been dancing for a while now, since I was about nine years old. The reason I thought of the dance classes as a way to improve my neighborhood is because I believe that kids do what they do because they have nothing better to do. The main problem in my area is street crime. In my opinion, this all stems from having nothing to do—these aren't bad kids—they do this as a kind of entertainment, because there's nothing else around or they don't know where to look. The dance classes will give them something to do at night, and we can start performing at shows. The aim is to get people off the street."

1 Reading

Read *Teenagers who make a difference* on page 36 and answer the questions.

Which of the teenagers ...

1 are particularly interested in helping young people in their own country?

...................., ...

2 started a campaign after something happened to a family member? ....

3 come from an area where crime is a problem for young people?

...................., ...

4 appeared on television? ....

5 hopes to stop teenagers becoming involved in crime by giving them something else to do? ....

6 thinks changing what young people wear can make a difference to their behavior? ....

7 wants to give teenagers something for free?

....

8 have received help from the music industry?

...................., ...

9 was influenced by an experience they had in another country? ....

2 Reading

Read the text again and match the beginnings with the endings.

1 Stacey realized how fortunate she was ☐
2 Stacey became interested in campaigning for poor people after ☐
3 Teenagers stole a cell phone ☐
4 When Stacey and the others went to India ☐
5 Stacey gave up her job ☐
6 Both Stacey and James ☐
7 Wacky ☐
8 Don Peterson ☐

a from James's brother.
b won a contest.
c have been involved in producing clothing.
d in order to become a campaigner.
e she appeared in a TV series.
f when she saw working conditions for teenagers in India.
g was a victim of bullying.
h they had to work in a clothing factory.

3 Vocabulary

Find words in the text that mean the same as these words and phrases.

1 interested in fashion ....
2 lucky ....
3 rich ....
4 make better ....
5 money to run a project ....
6 difficult ....
7 treating other people badly, especially those younger or weaker than you ....
8 started ....
9 incidents where people steal things on the street ....
10 give publicity to something ....

4 Vocabulary

Compare the words in list A with the words in list B. Write *S* if they have almost the same meaning, *O* if they are opposites, and *G* if A is more general than B.

	A	B	
1	crime	theft	*G*
2	poverty	wealth	
3	clothes	T-shirts	
4	goal	aim	
5	enormous	small	
6	launch	begin	
7	upset	happy	

5 Writing

Write a paragraph about the problems teenagers have in your country. Suggest ways in which these problems could be solved.

4 GETTING IT RIGHT

1 Some things won't have changed

1 Reading

Read about Zak. Then write sentences about what he will and won't be doing tomorrow.

Hi, I'm Zak. It's my last day at school today, and tomorrow I start my summer job. I'm working for a new chicken restaurant. I'm going to dress up as a chicken and persuade people to come into the restaurant. I'm getting up at seven in the morning because I start work at nine, and it takes a long time to put on the chicken clothes. I have lunch at two. (Guess what! Chicken!) From three to five I walk around the streets telling people about the restaurant. Then, at five, I work as a waiter in the restaurant (still dressed as a chicken). I finish work at seven and go home. Then I think I'll fall asleep immediately—guess what I'll dream about!

TODAY

7 a.m. Zak is sleeping.
9 a.m. Zak is arriving at school.
2 p.m. Zak is having an English class
4 p.m. Zak is playing soccer.
6 p.m. Zak is doing his homework.
8 p.m. Zak is watching TV.

TOMORROW

Zak won't be sleeping at seven o'clock tomorrow. He'll be getting up.

2 Future perfect

Read about Zak's life today and tomorrow in exercise 1 again. Then write sentences about what he will and won't have done by midnight tomorrow.

1 go to school/dress as a chicken

   He won't have gone to school, but he will have dressed as a chicken.

2 have chicken for lunch/have an English class

3 play soccer/walk around the streets

4 work as a waiter/do his homework

5 watch TV/dream about chicken

6 earn some money/have a quiet day

38

UNIT 4

3 Future perfect

Write questions and answer them.

1 Zak sleeps for eight hours a day.
   How many hours will he have slept
   five days from now? *Forty.*

2 Zak eats two chicken burgers a day.
   _____
   ten days from now? _____

3 Zak washes his chicken costume every day.
   _____
   a week from now? _____

4 Zak earns $80 a day.
   _____
   two days from now? _____

5 The Happy Chickenburger restaurant sells 300 burgers a day.
   _____
   a week from now? _____

6 Zak doesn't have time to watch TV.
   _____
   three days from now? _____

4 Future progressive and future perfect

Complete with the future progressive or future perfect of the verbs.

Future Perfect?

What will the future be like? Are we facing a bright new world or one which is going from bad to worse? Not surprisingly, futurologists, experts who predict the future, disagree. Some say that we (**1**) _____ (discover) new sources of energy 50 years from now and (**2**) _____ (enjoy) ourselves in wonderful new houses. At home and in factories and offices, robots (**3**) _____ (do) all the work. This means that everyone (**4**) _____ (stop) working and life will be one long vacation. However, 24-hour leisure brings its own problems, so experts predict that we (**5**) _____ (argue) with each other just as much, and in fact will be no happier than we are now. Other futurologists see a darker picture: people (**6**) _____ (live) crowded together in dirty cities, and their life expectancy (**7**) _____ (fall). We (**8**) _____ (use) up all our energy resources, and because of global warming the sea level (**9**) _____ (rise) more and more each year. Since experts never agree about anything, I think they (**10**) _____ (discuss) what the future will be like for many years to come!

5 Vocabulary

Complete the sentences with the correct form of these verbs to make phrasal verbs with *out*.

| carry   figure   miss   point   wipe |

1 I realized what was wrong when she _____ out my mistake.

2 The soldier _____ out his orders.

3 It took Zak a long time to _____ out how much he had earned.

4 Zak worked all summer, so he _____ out on a vacation.

5 It's important that we _____ out diseases like malaria.

6 Vocabulary

Match the words in list A with the words in list B and write seven compound nouns.

A	B	
1 house	chip	1 *household*
2 life	problems	2 _____
3 micro	energy	3 _____
4 nuclear	expectancy	4 _____
5 pulse	hold	5 _____
6 health	technology	6 _____
7 wireless	rate	7 _____

7 Pronunciation

Write the number of syllables and mark the stress.

advance *2*   combine ____   executive ____

expectancy ____   indication ____   microchip ____

obtainable ____   researcher ____   retirement ____

vaccine ____   wireless ____

> **Extension** Look at the times in exercise 1. Write sentences saying what you will be doing at these times tomorrow. Then imagine it is midnight tomorrow. Write more sentences saying what you will and won't have done by then.

39

4 GETTING IT RIGHT
2 We won't halt global warming until …

1 Reading

Read and complete the text with these words.

atmosphere emissions greenhouse solution
take travel unless whenever will won't

THE TRUTH ABOUT CARBON OFFSETS

"For every problem there is a (1) _____ which is simple, clean, and wrong."
H. L. Mencken, journalist (1850–1956)

There are two kinds of carbon: active carbon, which moves naturally between forests, oceans, and the (2) _____, and carbon which is locked away under the ground in coal, oil, and gas. When we burn coal, oil, and gas, we permit carbon dioxide, a (3) _____ gas, to escape into the air. Some people say we should plant trees to offset our carbon (4) _____, but if we do this, we (5) _____ put carbon back under the ground. Carbon dioxide, which trees take from the atmosphere, can return to the air through fire, disease, or when trees are cut down. Carbon underground will stay there (6) _____ we dig it up and burn it.

We must (7) _____ the world energy crisis seriously, but carbon offsets alone are not enough. For a start, no one is really sure of the answer to the question, "If I fly from A to B, how much carbon dioxide (8) _____ my flight produce?" Different organizations give different figures. So what should we do? The answer is simple, clean, and right: (9) _____ you plan to go somewhere by plane, ask yourself, "Is there another way I could (10) _____ ?"

2 First conditional

Rewrite what Ali and Jo said, choosing *if* or *unless*, and putting the verbs in the correct tense.

1 ALI If/Unless you (promise) to listen carefully, I (explain) about carbon emissions.
If you promise to listen carefully, I'll explain about carbon emissions.

2 JO If/Unless you (explain) clearly, I (not understand) what you mean.
_____

3 ALI If/Unless you (fly), you (damage) the environment.
_____

4 JO If/Unless I (fly), I (not have) much time with my friends.
_____

5 ALI (it/matter) if/unless you (not go) at all?
_____

6 JO My friends (be) disappointed if/unless I (not visit) them.
_____

7 ALI Your friends (understand) if/unless you (explain) why you can't come.
_____

8 ALI If/Unless you (go) by train, I (come) with you.
_____

40

UNIT 4

3 First conditional

Complete with *if* or *unless* and put the verbs in the correct tense.

1 People ___will continue___ (continue) to fly ___unless___ train travel ___becomes___ (become) much cheaper.

2 _____ railroad companies _____ (want) more people to travel by train, they _____ (have to) improve schedule information.

3 There _____ (be) floods in parts of Manhattan _____ the sea level _____ (rise).

4 _____ big organizations _____ (do) something about climate change now, it _____ (be) too late.

5 Many people don't believe it _____ (make) any difference _____ they _____ (fly).

6 _____ business people _____ (have) video conferences more often, they _____ (not need) to travel so much.

7 _____ air travel _____ (decrease), global temperatures _____ (continue) to increase.

8 Soon we _____ (have to) pay a special carbon tax _____ we _____ (travel) by air.

4 Future time clauses with *when, as soon as* and *until*

Complete the sentences with the simple present or simple future.

1 I _____ (go) swimming as soon as school _____ (finish).

2 She _____ (not decide) what to wear until she _____ (listen) to the weather forecast.

3 They _____ (be) in touch when they _____ (know) what their plans are.

4 He _____ (laugh) when he _____ (hear) that joke.

5 Until you _____ (pass) the test, you _____ (not be) allowed to drive the car by yourself.

6 I _____ (call) you as soon as I _____ (hear) from her.

5 Future time clauses with *when, as soon as*, and *until*

Complete with *when, as soon as*, or *until*.

1 I know it's very important, so I'll call you _____ I arrive.

2 Don't forget to buy milk _____ you go to the supermarket.

3 You will have to wait _____ I finish my dinner.

4 _____ I see you, I'll tell you what I've decided.

5 You know that I'll call you _____ I can.

6 I won't be able to drive you _____ I get my driver's license.

6 Vocabulary

Match the verbs in list A with the words and phrases in list B. Then write the phrases.

	A		B		
1	fund		a problem	1	*fund a project*
2	plant		action	2	_____
3	reduce		a project	3	_____
4	solve		the impact	4	_____
5	take		together	5	_____
6	work		trees	6	_____

7 Vocabulary

Match these words and phrases with their definitions.

carbon dioxide   drought   energy crisis   flood   global warming

1 increase in the temperature of the Earth

_____

2 gas which comes from burning oil _____

3 lots of water which covers land that was dry before

_____

4 long period of time without rain _____

5 serious problem with power supplies _____

8 Pronunciation

Write the number of syllables and mark the stress.

■
atmosphere _3_ balance _____ campaigner _____

crisis _____ emission _____ energy _____

organization _____ unless _____ whenever _____

> **Extension** Write a list of ways we can take action to cut carbon emissions and reduce the impact of global warming.

41

3 If you could choose ...

1 Reading

A friend of Vic Gerrard's named Ben wants to go to Nepal. Vic asked Ben what he would do if he had problems there. Read the conversation, complete each question, and match it with one of the pictures A–F.

VIC So, Ben, you would like to be in Nepal now, wouldn't you? (**1**) But what would you do if there _____*was*_____ (be) a lot of snow when you were there?   **1** ☐

BEN I'd dig a hole and hide in it.

VIC (**2**) And what would you do if you _____ (eat) something which made you sick?   **2** ☐

BEN I think I'd go to bed and drink lots of water.

VIC (**3**) How about if you _____ (meet) someone you liked, but couldn't understand what they said—what would you do?   **3** ☐

BEN I'd use sign language.

VIC That's a good idea. You'd probably make lots of friends there. (**4**) What would you do if they all _____ (decide) to come and stay in your room until late at night?   **4** ☐

BEN I'd sleep under the bed!

VIC That wouldn't be very comfortable! Now, you have to be careful with your money when you are traveling. (**5**) What would you do if a pickpocket _____ (steal) all your money?   **5** ☐

BEN Well, I'd probably borrow some money from a friend.

VIC I see. (**6**) What would you do if you _____ (lose) your plane ticket as well?   **6** ☐

BEN I'd travel back overland.

UNIT 4

2 Second conditional

Complete with the simple past or *would*, and answer the questions.

1 Who _would you speak_ (you/speak) to if you
wanted (want) help with a problem?
I'd speak to my sister.

2 What _____ (you/say) if a rich uncle
_____ (give) you a lot of money for your
birthday?

3 What _____ (you/do) if you
_____ (find) a big spider in your bed?

4 If you _____ (can) meet a famous movie
star, which star _____ (it/be)?

5 If you _____ (can) have one wish, what
_____ (it/be)?

6 Who _____ (you/ask) if you
_____ (need) to borrow some money?

7 What _____ (you/miss) most if you
_____ (have) to spend a year on a
desert island?

3 Second conditional

Write sentences using the second conditional.

1 You don't listen, so we argue all the time.
If you listened, we wouldn't argue all the time.

2 We don't have a map, so we don't know where to go.

3 She complains all the time, so people ignore her.

4 I bike to school, so I don't spend money on bus fares.

5 He talks to everyone, so he doesn't finish his work.

6 We like the singer, so we buy tickets for all her concerts.

4 *wish/if only* + simple past

Complete with the correct form of these verbs.

> be   can   grow   have   know   not feel   not like   shine

1 I wish I _____ able to swim.

2 If only money _____ on trees.

3 She wishes she _____ longer hair.

4 If only I _____ drive.

5 He wishes he _____ so tired.

6 If only I _____ their address.

7 I wish I _____ chocolate so much.

8 If only the sun _____ every day.

5 Vocabulary

Match these words and phrases with their definitions.

> in theory   magical   pace   paradise
> scenery   traditional   trekking

1 wonderful, with mystery _____

2 natural things you can see in a place
_____

3 going on a long and difficult walk _____

4 a perfect place _____

5 following the way people have usually done things
_____

6 speed _____

7 opposite of *in practice* _____

6 Pronunciation

Do they rhyme (✓) or not (✗)?

1 wish   rich | ✗ |
2 guest   best | |
3 hostel   coastal | |
4 choose   lose | |
5 tea   knee | |
6 could   wood | |
7 pace   days | |
8 trek   break | |

> **Extension** Where would you live if you could choose to live anywhere in the world? Write a paragraph about where you would go and what you would do.

43

4 GETTING IT RIGHT

4 Integrated Skills
Debating an issue

1 Reading

Read the text and complete with these words.

> able agree animals arguing damage danger difference example flights freedom
> guesthouse only overland partly result stealing strongly thirdly transportation wars

For and against backpacking

We asked two experienced backpackers, Jo and Ali, about the good and bad sides of independent travel.

Jo: Backpacking is great—it gives you the (1) _____ to go where you want, when you want. The first good thing about backpacking is that it's cheap. Young people don't have a lot of money, but they often have plenty of time. So they can travel (2) _____ cheaply and slowly. Secondly, because we use the local public (3) _____ system, we're (4) _____ to get much closer to the lives of ordinary people. If you're on an old bus full of local farmers and their (5) _____, you'll find out far more about the country than if you're on a modern tourist bus. If more people got to know other countries in this way, there'd be fewer (6) _____ in the world. Thirdly, because we visit remote parts of the world, we bring much-needed money to poor areas. For (7) _____, we buy food in local markets and fish direct from the fishermen, so our money goes directly into local society. And finally, backpackers are environmentally friendly travelers—we use very few resources and we don't (8) _____ the places we visit. We don't need huge concrete hotels—living in a tent or staying in a simple (9) _____ is fine for us.

Ali: I'm not sure that I (10) _____, and I think that there's a real (11) _____ that backpackers can destroy what they've come thousands of kilometers to see. First of all, many backpackers have a kind of "check-the-box" approach to travel—been there, seen that, bought the T-shirt. They collect countries like stamps, and want to visit as many as possible. If (12) _____ more people were happy to get to know a few places well, rather than lots of places a little. Secondly, there really isn't much (13) _____ between backpackers and package tourists. Backpackers often have little real contact with the countries they visit because they travel together in a closed world of cheap (14) _____, hostels, Internet cafés, and beach parties. They all read the same guidebooks and, as a (15) _____, they go to the same places. (16) _____, I really don't like the way many backpackers use cameras. I read somewhere that it's called "taking" a picture because what you're really doing is (17) _____ it! I wish people asked permission before photographing someone. Fourthly, and I know this is (18) _____ because backpackers don't have much money, but it really annoys me when they try to pay as little as possible for things. They spend hours (19) _____ with a poor person over the price of something just to save a few cents. Not all backpackers are like this, of course, but these are four things which I feel (20) _____ about.

2 Writing

Read the text again and make a list in your notebook of four advantages and four disadvantages of backpacking.

44

3 Writing

Use your list from exercise 2 to write two short paragraphs summarizing the advantages and disadvantages of backpacking.

4 Crossword

Complete the crossword puzzle.

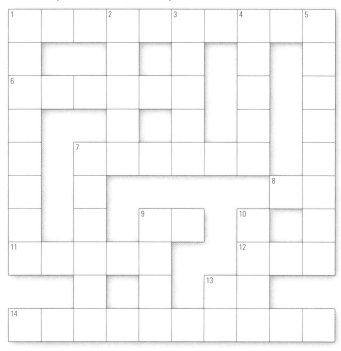

Across →

1. Air around the Earth and other planets. (10)
6. Involving the whole world. (6)
7. Road in a town. (6)
8. No one wants to miss out … a chance. (2)
9. People shouldn't fly … much. (2)
11. If you're afraid of falling, hold on … (5)
12. Simple past of *eat*. (3)
13. On vacation, you can live life … a slower pace. (2)
14. When people stop working, usually at 60 or 65. (10)

Down ↓

1. Discussion which is sometimes angry. (8)
2. Go around a large object in space. (5)
3. Rate of heartbeat, usually felt at the wrist. (5)
4. Choose a representative by voting for them. (5)
5. Facts that help to prove something. (8)
7. It will be mostly sunny tomorrow, but there's a … chance of rain. (6)
9. Bright light in the night sky, not a planet. (4)
10. Speed at which something happens. (4)
13. Opposite of *p.m.* (2)

LEARNER INDEPENDENCE

Discussion and debate

Two important skills are *Asking for repetition* (A) and *Checking you've understood* (C). Write *A* or *C* after these expressions.

1. I'm sorry, I didn't catch that. ....
2. Can you go over that again, please? ....
3. So what you mean is … ....
4. Unless I've misunderstood, what you're saying is … ....
5. Would you mind saying that again, please? ....
6. In other words, you think … ....
7. What you're getting at is … ....
8. Sorry, I didn't follow that. ....
9. So your point is … ....

Extensive reading

Read an English book and choose a picture that you like. Write a paragraph describing the picture, and say what happened just before and after the event in the picture.

4 GETTING IT RIGHT
Inspired EXTRA!

CONSOLIDATION

LESSON 1

Complete with the future progressive or future perfect of the verbs.

1 She drinks a glass of juice every morning. How many glasses of juice will she *have drunk* (drink) a week from now?

2 Your flight gets in at 12. We _____ (wait) for you at the airport.

3 I don't know what I _____ (do) on Tuesday, so I'm not sure when we can meet.

4 She _____ (finish) her exams by the end of June.

5 In a few days he _____ (learn) how to use his new laptop.

6 They _____ (spend) next summer in Florida.

7 How long _____ you _____ (use) the tennis court? We'd like to play after you.

8 Unless we stop him, he _____ (eat) all the chocolate in the box!

LESSON 2

Write sentences using the first conditional with both *if* and *unless*.

1 they/run/they/miss the bus
   If they don't run, they'll miss the bus.
   Unless they run, they'll miss the bus.

2 she/save enough money/she/able to afford a new coat

3 he/ask me/I/tell him the answer to the puzzle

4 you/hurry/you/be late for school

5 we/wait in line/we/get tickets for the concert

LESSON 3

Put the words in the right order to complete the sentences.

1 what help wouldn't do I knew ask for to I
   If _____

2 local time enough language she she'd learn the had
   If _____

3 understood home my I late why came father only
   If _____

4 phone remember her only I number could
   If _____

5 could to you you live like where choose would
   If _____?

LESSON 4

Match these words and phrases with their definitions.

1 be in favor of
2 motion
3 opponent
4 oppose
5 propose
6 sum up
7 vote

a decide something or choose a representative in an election
b topic of a debate
c summarize
d support
e be against
f put forward a motion in a debate
g someone who is against you in a debate or competition

Spelling

Read and complete the words from Unit 4.

The sound /s/ is usually written *s* (e.g., *pulse*) but in some words it is spelled *c* (e.g., *balance*).

1 advan__e 2 de__ision 3 decrea__e 4 ca__e
5 __ertain 6 cri__is 7 democra__y 8 differen__e
9 expectan__y 10 off__et 11 pa__e 12 produ__e
13 publi__ity 14 ra__e 15 __lightest 16 violen__e

Brainteaser

What would you say if you met a monster with three heads?

Answer on page 49.

46

UNIT 4

EXTENSION

LESSON 1

Write four sentences about what you will be doing next Saturday at 10 a.m., 2 p.m., 6 p.m., and 9 p.m., and four sentences about what you will have done over the weekend by next Sunday evening.

At 10 a.m. next Saturday

By Sunday evening

LESSON 2

Complete the sentences using the first conditional and the verbs and phrases.

1 If I pass my exams this summer, I _____ (be able to)

2 Unless it stops raining soon, we _____ (have to)

3 If everyone comes to the party, we _____ (need to)

4 Unless I do my laundry soon, I _____ (not have)

5 If you don't hurry, you _____ (be late for)

6 Unless you read the letter, you _____ (not know)

7 If you want to go skiing, you _____ (have to)

8 Unless you listen, you _____ (not understand)

LESSON 3

Imagine you are these people and complete their wishes using the simple past.

1 *The richest person in the world*: I wish _____

2 *The poorest person in the world*: I wish _____

3 *Someone lost in the desert*: If only _____

4 *An actor about to go on stage*: I wish _____

5 *A soccer player who has just lost a game*: If only _____

6 *The loneliest person in the world*: I wish _____

LESSON 4

Look at exercise 7 on page 55 of the Student's Book and write two paragraphs discussing arguments for and against one of the topics which you didn't choose for your class debate.

Web watch

Greenpeace is an environmental campaign group. Do an Internet search for *greenpeace.org* and follow the link to the *Greenpeace* website. Find out what campaigns they are involved in right now. Which ones are important to you and why? Discuss the issues with a partner, and rank the campaigns in order of importance.

Spelling

Read and complete the words from Unit 4.

The sound /ʃ/ is often written *sh* (e.g., *ship*). It can be also be written *t* (e.g., *fiction*). And in some words /ʃ/ is written with *c* or *ss* (e.g., *delicious, profession*).

1 ac___ion   2 addi___ion   3 cla___   4 cru___ial   5 emi___ion

6 expre___ion   7 i___ue   8 mo___ion   9 organiza___ion

10 politi___ian   11 ra___ial   12 relation___ip   13 wi___

Brainteaser

An explorer left his camp and walked 500 meters south before turning west. After walking 500 meters in this direction, he saw a bear. He was so frightened that he ran 500 meters north—and found himself back at his camp.

What color was the bear?

Answer on page 49.

47

REVIEW
UNITS 3–4

1 Read the text. For each number 1–15, choose word or phrase A, B, C, or D.

Futurologists' predictions for the 21st Century

Who would want to be a futurologist in our rapidly changing world? Technological advances are developing so (**1**) _____ quickly that most predictions are out of date the day after they're made. Things are moving (**2**) _____ that predictions are becoming more and more extreme. A futurologist recently claimed that by 2015, a quarter of TV celebrities (**3**) _____ robots. Hard to believe, even though some of the human ones today are quite robot-like! A more interesting prediction is that by 2017, robot-teachers (**4**) _____ better results than human teachers. What a surprise to learn that by then, robot-teachers (**5**) _____ common! When (**6**) _____ the first robot-student, I wonder? An even bigger surprise: it's predicted that by the 2020s, technology (**7**) _____ chimpanzees and dolphins who are as intelligent as humans. Medical science is developing (**8**) _____ rapidly, and it's said that by 2015, surgeons (**9**) _____ plastic bones regularly in operations. And unless the predictions are wrong, we (**10**) _____ artificial brains by 2040. If we could trust the predictions, we (**11**) _____ to plan our lives better. For example, it's predicted that 60% of the world's population will be living in cities by 2015. So is it time to think about moving to the country? I wish I (**12**) _____. If only predicting the future (**13**) _____ as easy as reading about the past. It's quite likely that by 2015 we (**14**) _____ most of our music online. But who can believe that by the same time we (**15**) _____ to dance with robot dance-teachers?

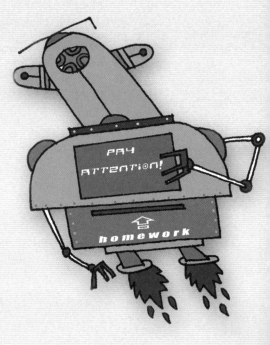

1	**A** incredible	**B** incredibly	**C** more incredibly	**D** most incredibly
2	**A** fast	**B** so fast	**C** faster	**D** fastest
3	**A** are	**B** are being	**C** be	**D** will be
4	**A** are getting	**B** were getting	**C** will have gotten	**D** will be getting
5	**A** are becoming	**B** became	**C** will become	**D** will have become
6	**A** do we see	**B** did we see	**C** are we seeing	**D** will we see
7	**A** creates	**B** created	**C** has created	**D** will have created
8	**A** equal	**B** equally	**C** more equally	**D** most equally
9	**A** are using	**B** will have used	**C** will be using	**D** have been using
10	**A** will have	**B** will have had	**C** will be having	**D** have been having
11	**A** are able	**B** will be able	**C** were able	**D** would be able
12	**A** know	**B** knew	**C** have known	**D** will know
13	**A** is	**B** will	**C** has been	**D** were
14	**A** buy	**B** are buying	**C** will buy	**D** will have bought
15	**A** learn	**B** are learning	**C** have learned	**D** will be learning

2 Complete with the correct form of the words in capitals.

1	The life _____ in some developing countries is very low.	EXPECT
2	Will fresh food be easily _____ in the future?	OBTAIN
3	She is looking forward to learning to paint after her _____.	RETIRE
4	The bank is a big _____ so I don't know who to contact.	ORGANIZE
5	Tomorrow we're going to elect a class _____.	REPRESENT
6	He was one of our _____ in the basketball competition.	OPPOSE
7	I saw an anti-pollution _____ on the TV news.	DEMONSTRATE
8	Paris is a _____ city—everyone loves it.	MAGIC

48

3 Complete the second sentence so that it means the same as the first sentence.

1 Lightning travels more slowly than light.
  Light _____

2 The two astronauts who first walked on the Moon were Neil Armstrong and Buzz Aldrin.
  Neil Armstrong and Buzz Aldrin _____

3 The dive was so deep that they didn't expect to see any fish.
  They didn't expect _____

4 The two-hour flight will cost each passenger $200,000.
  Each passenger _____

5 In 2050, we will kill the last whale.
  By 2050, we _____

6 If we don't do something about carbon emissions soon, it will be too late.
  Unless _____

7 Unless you answer my questions, I'll tell your parents.
  If _____

8 I'd go to Nepal if I had enough money.
  If _____

4 Find the word that is different.

1 expand   increase   reduce   rise
2 crisis   drought   earthquake   flood
3 debate   terrorism   violence   war
4 family   quickly   rapidly   slowly
5 operation   pasteurization   segregation   vaccination
6 create   destroy   generate   produce
7 rate   pace   speed   weight
8 flight   journey   trek   voyage

Answers to Brainteasers

UNIT 3
Consolidation The future.
Extension The Moon.

UNIT 4
Consolidation Hello, hello, hello!
Extension White—the man was at the North Pole.

LEARNER INDEPENDENCE
SELF ASSESSMENT

Vocabulary

1 Draw this chart in your notebook. How many words can you write in each category?

More than 10? Good!   *More than 12?* Very good!
More than 15? Excellent!

Space flight	
Global warming	
Tourism and travel	

2 Put the words in order to make expressions from the phrasebooks in Lesson 4 in Units 3 and 4.

1 sight fantastic a what
   What a fantastic sight!

2 does what this have with do to …
   _____

3 thing the is incredible most …
   _____

4 is the point whole …
   _____

5 people that like only were if …
   _____

6 ages takes it
   _____

7 tell will time only
   _____

8 sounds it silly
   _____

Check your answers.
8/8 Excellent!   *6/8* Very good!   *4/8* Try again!

My learning diary
In Units 3 and 4:
My favorite topic is _____

My favorite picture is _____

The three lessons I like most are _____

My favorite activity or exercise is _____

Something I don't understand is _____

Something I want to learn more about is _____

49

5 EXTRAORDINARY PEOPLE

1 If the ship hadn't hit an iceberg ...

1 Reading

Read the text and complete it with these words.

> bigger   check   can   dictionaries   estimated   extraordinary
> heard   known   users   surf   world   wouldn't

Alexander Graham Bell invented the first practical telephone in 1876. But if you had told him then that one day people would carry his invention in their pockets, he (1) _____ have believed you. Equally, when phone companies started putting up phone lines and installing telephones in people's homes, they could not have (2) _____ what they were starting. They would have been very surprised to see modern phones with no wires, which are so light that people (3) _____ carry them around and use them wherever and whenever they want. Today, nobody really knows how many cell phones there are in the (4) _____. It is (5) _____ that there are at least five billion. But the number could be much (6) _____ than that, since around 80 million phones are sold every year in the U.S. alone. And the cell phone's impact on our lives has been (7) _____.

As well as making phone calls, we now take pictures, play music, watch movies, play games, and (8) _____ the Internet on our cell phones as if it were the most natural thing in the world. We (9) _____ the scores of sports games and the times of trains. We read and send e-mails, find definitions in online (10) _____, look up facts on Wikipedia®, and buy and sell on eBay™, which has 233 million (11) _____. Our cell phones are our cameras, our agendas, our photo albums, our shopping lists, our portable stereos. Who would have thought when Alexander Graham Bell's assistant (12) _____ that first crackly message down the phone line: "Watson, come here! I want to see you!" that one day all this would be possible!

An invention that changed the world

2 Third conditional

Write sentences using the third conditional about Sue's lucky day.

1 Sue/catch bus/she/not be late
   Sue would have caught the bus if she hadn't been late.

2 Sue/get wet/she/not open her umbrella
   _____

3 the car/hit Sue/she/cross the road a moment earlier
   _____

4 the piano/fall on Sue/she/not run for the bus
   _____

5 Sue/fall into the hole/Sam/not shout
   _____

6 Sam/call an ambulance/Sue/be hurt
   _____

50

UNIT 5

3 Third conditional

Write sentences using the third conditional.

1 Sue didn't say thank you to Sam because she was late.
Sue would have said thank you to Sam if she hadn't been late.

2 She didn't get a taxi because she didn't see one.

3 She was late for work because she didn't get a taxi.

4 Sue's boss was mad at her because she wasn't on time.

5 Sue yelled at her boss because she didn't think about the consequences.

6 She lost her job because she yelled at her boss.

4 *wish/if only* + past perfect

Rewrite the sentences using the words in parentheses.

1 What a shame I missed the show. (wish)
I wish I hadn't missed the show.

2 He didn't remember to mail the package. (if only)

3 You shouldn't have said that. (wish)

4 She didn't call and apologize. (if only)

5 I'm sorry I broke your camera. (wish)

6 I didn't know the right thing to say. (if only)

7 She regrets not reading the instruction book first. (wish)

8 What a shame they weren't at the party. (if only)

5 Vocabulary

Match these words with their definitions.

binoculars   disaster   drill   iceberg   freeze   lookout

1 become extremely cold

2 a way of learning something by practicing many times

3 equipment that lets you see distant objects clearly

4 someone who is responsible for looking out for danger

5 something very bad that happens

6 a very large piece of ice floating in the ocean

6 Vocabulary

Compare the words in list A with the words in list B. Write *S* if they have almost the same meaning, *O* if they are opposites, and *G* if A is more general than B.

	A	B	
1	crew	team	*S*
2	journey	voyage	
3	reduce	increase	
4	lose	save	
5	family	brother	
6	full	empty	
7	boat	lifeboat	
8	extraordinary	remarkable	

7 Pronunciation

Write the number of syllables and mark the stress.

binoculars *4*   direction ____   disaster ____

extraordinary ____   lookout ____   passenger ____

reduced ____   survivor ____   unsinkable ____

Extension Write a paragraph about an invention which you think changed the world. Who invented it and when? How did it change the world? Was it for better or for worse?

51

5 EXTRAORDINARY PEOPLE
2 You have to be careful

1 Reading
Read the text and complete it with the correct form of the verbs.

Sayings from around the world

In Poland they say: "A good painter (**1**) _____ (need to) give his picture a title, but a bad painter (**2**) _____ (must)." A saying in many countries is: "You (**3**) _____ (have to) take the good with the bad." In Russia they say: "You (**4**) _____ (need to) have 100 roubles but you (**5**) _____ (need to) have 100 friends." In Spain they say: "You (**6**) _____ (have to) make the most of the chances you get." Another Spanish saying is: "Good men (**7**) _____ (must) die, but death cannot kill their names." A well-known American saying comes from Mark Twain: "If you tell the truth, you (**8**) _____ (have to) remember anything." Another is from Bob Dylan: "You (**9**) _____ (have to) be a weather man to know which way the wind blows." The British say: "You (**10**) _____ (must) learn to walk before you can run." And finally, another British saying: "If you are lazy now, you will (**11**) _____ (have to) work harder later."

2 *have to*, *don't have to*, and *can't*
Complete with *have to*, *don't have to*, or *can't*.

1 You _*have to*_ be over 18 to get into the club.
2 You _____ cross the road when the light is red.
3 You _____ be able to swim to take up water skiing.
4 You _____ be a genius to do well on the quiz. It's easy!
5 You _____ believe everything you read in the papers.
6 You _____ wait for me. I know the way.
7 You _____ be physically fit to be a diver.
8 You _____ smoke in public places.
9 You _____ have a driver's license to work in a store.
10 You _____ have good qualifications to earn a living.

UNIT 5

3 had to/didn't have to and needed to/ didn't need to

Complete with the correct past form of the verbs.

1 They said I _didn't need to_ (need to) bring any food to the party, but I decided to take a cake anyway.

2 We _____ (have to) wait for hours at the airport until the check-in opened.

3 He _____ (have to) pay anything for the CDs—they were a gift.

4 It wasn't really necessary, but I just felt that I _____ (need to) check that the door was locked.

5 She felt she _____ (need to) talk to her best friend before deciding.

6 He didn't know that he _____ (have to) have a ticket before he got on the train.

7 They _____ (have to) be very careful with money after their expensive vacation.

8 She was only away for two days, so she _____ (need to) take a big suitcase.

4 need and need to

Complete with the correct form of *need* or *need to*.

1 I'm very tired. I really _need_ a vacation.

2 I _____ go somewhere hot and sunny.

3 I _____ very little when I'm on vacation—just sun, sand, and the ocean.

4 It _____ be anywhere expensive or fancy.

5 I just _____ chill out and relax.

6 So if you don't hear from me you _____ worry. I'll be on the beach.

7 If you _____ contact me, you can leave a message on my cell phone.

8 In fact, you look as if you _____ a break, too. Why don't you come with me?

5 Vocabulary

Match the verbs in list A with the words and phrases in list B. Then write the phrases.

	A	B		
1	be	a disease	1	_be careful_
2	treat	careful	2	
3	get	calm	3	
4	see	clearly	4	
5	stay	to know	5	

6 Vocabulary

Match the words in list A with the words in list B and write eight compound nouns.

	A	B		
1	driver's	attendant	1	_driver's license_
2	snake	attraction	2	
3	flight	license	3	
4	guide	style	4	
5	hair	lines	5	
6	tourist	venom	6	

7 Vocabulary

Compare the words in list A with the words in list B. Write *S* if they have almost the same meaning, *O* if they are opposites, and *G* if A is more general than B.

	A	B	
1	boat	yacht	_G_
2	diploma	degree	
3	grin	smile	
4	elaborate	complicated	
5	well-fed	starving	
6	lately	recently	
7	undamaged	broken	
8	calm	nervous	
9	guidelines	rules	

8 Pronunciation

Do they rhyme (✓) or not (✗)?

1	crew	two	✓
2	calm	farm	☐
3	yacht	hot	☐
4	shower	lower	☐
5	diving	living	☐
6	file	style	☐
7	scary	carry	☐
8	flight	height	☐
9	wax	walks	☐
10	jar	war	☐

Extension Write a paragraph about your ideal job. What do you have to do in this job? What don't you have to do?

53

5 EXTRAORDINARY PEOPLE

3 What could have happened to them?

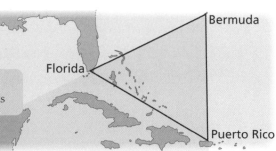

1 Reading

Read the text and complete it with these words.

> although crashed crew disappearance flew have however later
> lights may mid-air part pulled sailing sent solo take-off wrecks

The Bermuda Triangle

Maritime experts are extremely puzzled by the Bermuda Triangle—the area of ocean between Bermuda, Florida, and Puerto Rico—because many ships have disappeared there. The first reference to the area was by Christopher Columbus in the fifteenth century. Columbus and his crew saw "strange dancing (1) _____" in the sky and reported problems with their compass. At another time, they saw what might (2) _____ been a falling star.

Captain Joshua Slocum in his boat *Spray* was the first man to sail (3) _____ around the world in the 1890s, but he was never heard of again after (4) _____ into the Bermuda Triangle in 1909. Nine years (5) _____, a U.S. Navy ship *Cyclops* and her (6) _____ of 309 men were lost in the Triangle, (7) _____ they had the latest radio equipment. While the radio equipment (8) _____ have failed, this doesn't explain the ship's (9) _____. And in 1944, Captain Joe Talley nearly drowned when his fishing boat was (10) _____ underwater.

Ships are not the only things to disappear in the Triangle. In 1945, Flight 19, a group of five U.S. Navy planes, left Florida and (11) _____ into the Triangle. (12) _____, they were led by an officer with a history of getting lost and were soon off course. A huge flying boat was (13) _____ to find the missing planes, but radio contact was lost 20 minutes after (14) _____, and the flying boat exploded in (15) _____ over the Triangle. Although hundreds of planes and boats took (16) _____ in the search for the six planes and their crews, nothing was found. While the planes must have (17) _____ somewhere in the Triangle, the strange thing is that no one has found their (18) _____.

2 must have, can't have, could/may/might have + past participle

Complete the sentences with the correct form of the verbs.

1 What might *have happened* (happen) to the ships and planes in the Bermuda Triangle?
2 Columbus's crew could _____ (make) a mistake when reading their compass.
3 Slocum was such an experienced sailor that he can't _____ (get) lost in the Bermuda Triangle.
4 Some people think that a whale might _____ (hit) the *Spray* or that a big ship might _____ (run) into it.
5 Others are sure that aliens must _____ (abduct) Slocum.
6 The *Cyclops* was such a big ship that it can't _____ (disappear) without a trace.
7 Fixing the *Cyclops*' radio might _____ (be) difficult, but the ship could _____ (return) to port in Bermuda.
8 The U.S. was at war in 1918, so an enemy ship may _____ (attack) the *Cyclops*.
9 Captain Talley was lucky—he might _____ (drown) when his boat was pulled underwater.
10 Flight 19 may _____ (run) out of fuel and _____ (crash) in the ocean.
11 The five planes might _____ (attempt) emergency landings in the ocean and then sunk.
12 No one understands how air traffic control could _____ (lose) contact with the huge flying boat so soon after take-off.

54

UNIT 5

3 *must have* and *can't have* + past participle

Complete with *must have* or *can't have* + past participle.

1 Something really unusual ___*must have happened*___ (happen) to Slocum. He ___*can't have disappeared*___ (disappear) without a trace.

2 Some people say that the *Cyclops* _____ (be) in the Bermuda Triangle because they haven't found a wreck there.

3 The *Cyclops'* radio _____ (fail) because there was no transmission before the disappearance.

4 Whatever it was that pulled Joe Talley's boat underwater _____ (be) incredibly powerful.

5 The pilots of Flight 19 _____ (get lost) all at the same time, even if they had a bad leader.

6 It is thought by some that the planes _____ (land) back in Florida, although they haven't been found.

7 There _____ (be) lots more missing boats and planes which we don't know about.

4 *must have* and *could/may/ might have* + past participle

Complete with the correct form of one of the verbs in parentheses.

1 It ___*must have been*___ your brother who called. I'm sure it was his voice. (must/could be)

2 It _____ better if you had waited until I was ready before starting the meal. (must/might be)

3 They _____ a mistake. This isn't what I ordered. (must/may make)

4 I don't know why he's late—I don't have a clue what _____ to him. (must/could happen)

5 You _____ that picture two years ago before we moved to New York. (must/might take)

6 I _____ wrong but I'm not sure and I'm not saying sorry. (must/may be)

7 I guess the call _____ from your sister, but it didn't sound like her at all. (must/might be)

8 Everything _____ a lot worse. Although it was raining, we got home before we were too wet. (must/could be)

5 Vocabulary

Complete the sentences with the correct form of these verbs to make phrasal verbs with *up*.

| blow end grow make sum take |

1 We didn't know where we were, so we _____ up asking the way.

2 Did the plane _____ up in mid-air? No one knows.

3 What do you want to be when you _____ up?

4 Is that story true or did he _____ it up?

5 Why don't you _____ up a musical instrument?

6 I'd like to _____ up what we have discussed.

6 Vocabulary

Match the words in list A with the words in list B and write six compound nouns.

A	**B**	
1 air	equipment	**1** *air traffic*
2 emergency	landing	**2** _____
3 radar	operation	**3** _____
4 radio	screen	**4** _____
5 search	storm	**5** _____
6 snow	traffic	**6** _____

7 Vocabulary

Complete with these words and phrases.

| a message   a record   a trip down a plane   out of fuel   up in a place |

1 break _____

2 end _____

3 take _____

4 run _____

5 send _____

6 shoot _____

8 Pronunciation

Write the number of syllables and mark the stress.

■
abduct __2__   attempt ____   disappeared ____

navigator ____   pioneer ____   snowstorm ____

speculation ____   transatlantic ____

> **Extension** Write a paragraph about one of the mysteries in this lesson or another that you know about. Say what you think happened.

55

5 EXTRAORDINARY PEOPLE

4 Integrated Skills
Contrasting facts and ideas

More extraordinary people

"I don't know why I have a connection with elephants; I just do," says Sangduen 'Lek' Chaillert. "When I was a child, my grandfather had an elephant to help him with work on the farm. His name was Thongkhum (meaning "Golden One") (**1**) _____. I've loved elephants ever since."

Lek (meaning "small" in Thai—and she is) was born in a remote mountain village in northern Thailand. Ten years ago, she started the Elephant Nature Park near where she was born (**2**) _____. Now there are 29 elephants of all ages, from babies to old male elephants living there. Some have been treated badly by their owners or injured by mines left from the war (**3**) _____. In towns, the elephants can't possibly receive the 200–300 kilos of food and 100–200 liters of water they need every day. The National Geographic Society has called Lek a "Hero for the Planet" because if she hadn't rescued these elephants, they would have died.

In 2011, Paul Freedman ran his 20th marathon, a 42-kilometer race around the city of London. Thousands of people take part in the marathon each year, so what made Paul different from other runners? The fact is that year he was 86, so (**4**) _____. He started running in the marathon at the age of 61 and, so far, he has raised more than $150,000 for charity. In 2008, he (**5**) _____ for his fundraising. Most of the money has gone to a hospice, where his wife Renee (**6**) _____. Paul trains (**7**) _____. His goal is to get to the finishing line in less than six hours! Do you think he will make it?

1 Reading

Read *More extraordinary people*. Then complete the text with seven of the phrases a–i. There are two extra phrases.

a while others are brought there from nearby towns
b met Queen Elizabeth, who gave him an award
c he was the oldest runner in the race
d by running 16 kilometers three times a week
e and he was like a member of the family
f died from lung cancer in 2007
g because everyone wanted to
h after an American had given her the land
i in which competitors run, swim, and cycle

2 Writing

Complete the sentences using information from the text.

1 Lek has loved elephants since _____

2 Two reasons elephants are brought to the Park are because _____

3 The elephants would have died if Lek _____

4 It's extraordinary that Paul ran in the 2011 London Marathon because _____

5 The money Paul raises goes to _____

6 Paul wants to complete _____

56

3 Crossword

Complete the crossword puzzle.

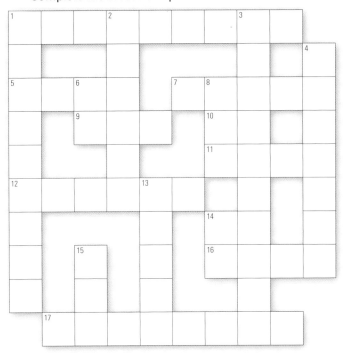

Across →

1 An … landing is when a plane has to land because of a problem. (9)
5 A top male soccer player was … $100,000 a month. (4)
7 The largest sea creature is the blue … (5)
9 I love playing soccer. It's really … (3)
10 No trace of Earhart … Noonan was found. (2)
11 Jeanette Ewart is … of a team. (4)
12 Scientists must … better batteries so electric vehicles can travel farther. (6)
14 If the *Titanic* hadn't hit an iceberg, … wouldn't have sunk. (2)
16 Amelia Earhart was never … again after her plane was lost. (4)
17 You need to … to stay healthy. (8)

Down ↓

1 Some mysteries can never be … (9)
2 When you slow down, you … your speed. (6)
3 Sharks, like people, all have different … (10)
4 When you are sure about something, you are … (7)
6 No one knows … Earhart and Noonan were spies. (2)
8 Do you like hip-… ? (3)
13 Most survivors wished they had … sailed on the *Titanic*. (5)
14 Mexico's star woman soccer player … known as "Marigol." (2)
15 When something breaks, you need to … it. (3)

LEARNER INDEPENDENCE

Using the Internet

A good way of expanding your vocabulary is to learn which words often go together. The Internet is an easy and powerful tool to help you find this out. Type the word(s) you want to find out about into a search engine (for phrases, choose *Advanced Search* and then "exact phrase"). For this unit, try these words and phrases:

character
injury
hit
luxury
physically
record-breaking
risk
run out of
transatlantic

You will get a lot of "hits," but you only need to look at a few and note down the interesting ones.

Extensive reading

Read an English book and write a new ending for the story. Think about what would/wouldn't have happened if things had been different.

5 EXTRAORDINARY PEOPLE

Inspired EXTRA!

CONSOLIDATION

LESSON 1

Rewrite the sentences using the third conditional.

1 You didn't ask me. I didn't help you.
If you had asked me, I would have helped you.

2 We didn't know what would happen. We opened the door.

3 She didn't have her phone. She didn't call him.

4 He knew that the water was deep. He dived in.

5 They didn't realize you were waiting. They were late.

LESSON 2

Complete with the correct verbs in parentheses.

1 This extra homework isn't compulsory so you
_____ (have to/don't have to) do it, but I
think you _____ (need to/don't need to)
do it to improve your English.

2 The law in this state says that you
_____ (have to/don't have to) be 17 to
drive a car.

3 I know I _____ (need to/don't need
to) say sorry, but I feel really bad about what I did so I
_____ (have to/don't have to) apologize.

4 We can choose our own hours at work: we
_____ (need to/don't need to) be there
at exactly 8 a.m. but we still _____
(have to/don't have to) work 35 hours a week.

5 You know the rules. You _____
(have to/don't have to) finish your work on time. You
_____ (need to/don't need to) bother
coming back next week.

LESSON 3

Respond using *must have* or *can't have* and the verbs in parentheses.

1 A: I waited for her outside the movie theater for an hour.
B: She _____ (forget)

2 A: I sent her a text but she didn't reply.
B: She _____ the text. (not get)

3 A: I had to wait a long time.
B: It _____ easy. (be)

4 A: No, it wasn't. But she called me today.
B: You _____ happy to hear from her. (be)

5 A: We're going to see the movie together tonight.
B: You _____ her! (forgive)

LESSON 4

Write questions for these answers about *"Is it a man's game?" asks Marigol.*

1 *How many goals has Maribel scored in
international games* ? 46.

2 _____ ? Nine

3 _____ ? 20

4 _____ ? 1999

Spelling

Correct the spelling of these words from Unit 5 by doubling one letter in each word.

1 afternon **2** anounce **3** atendant **4** canonball

5 confes **6** degr **7** disapear **8** dril

9 grining **10** lotery **11** mision **12** patern

13 pioner **14** profesional **15** trafic

Brainteaser

What question can never be answered by "Yes"?
Answer on page 73.

58

UNIT 5

EXTENSION

LESSON 1

Complete the sentences about events in your life using the third conditional.

1 If I had known

2 If someone had told me

3 If I had thought

4 If I had remembered

5 If I hadn't forgotten

LESSON 2

Complete the sentences for yourself.

1 When I'm at school I need to

2 When I was younger I didn't have to

3 At my school you don't have to

4 Something I don't need to worry about is

5 Last year I had to

6 The last time I needed to ask for help was

7 I know I don't have to, but I sometimes

8 At home we can't

LESSON 3

Complete using *must/can't/could/may/might have.*

1 Someone says you were rude to them at school yesterday. (You weren't at school.)
It *can't have been me.*

2 Your friend says you called her. (You didn't.)
It

3 Your teacher asks if it was your backpack that was left on the bus. (It wasn't.)
It

4 Your father says that you left the door open. (You can't remember if you did.)
It

5 A stranger asks if you dropped some money in the street. (You're not sure if the money is yours or not.)
It

6 A friend asks who your surprise birthday gift was from. (You don't know.)
It

LESSON 4

Write a paragraph about a famous sports star from your country.

Web watch

To find out more about the *Titanic*, type "story of the Titanic" into a search engine. Draw a timeline of the events.

Spelling

Complete the words from Unit 5 with *-ar, -er,* or *-or.*

1 charact_____   **2** disast_____   **3** div_____

4 doll_____   **5** hairdry_____   **6** juni_____

7 maj_____   **8** navigat_____   **9** neith_____

10 passeng_____   **11** pione_____   **12** popul_____

13 quart_____   **14** rad_____   **15** show_____

16 socc_____   **17** surviv_____   **18** wint_____

Brainteaser

What is it that comes four times in every week, two times in every month, but only once in a year?

Answer on page 73.

59

5 Culture

Saying the right thing

1 Reading

Who says what? Write the sentences in the boxes under the correct pictures.

A
- Can I see your driver's license, please?
- That's $5.15. I don't suppose you have the fifteen cents?
- Did you pack this bag yourself? Are you carrying anything for someone else?
- Are there any tickets left for the concert tonight?
- Could I have the check, please?
- I'd like to return these, please. They're the wrong size.

B
- No, it sold out weeks ago.
- Yes, of course. It was two coffees, wasn't it?
- I'm sorry, I don't have it with me.
- Yes, I did. And no, I'm not.
- No, I'm sorry, I don't.
- Do you have the receipt with you?

1

A:
B:

4

A:
B:

2

A:
B:

5

A:
B:

3

A:
B:

6

A:
B:

2 Reading

Emma and her boyfriend Andy are in a clothing store. Read and complete the dialogue with sentences a–h.

a   The fitting rooms are over there.
b   Do you have it in a smaller size?
c   No, thank you, we're just looking.
d   Excuse me, could I try this on, please?
e   How much are they?
f   I don't think it fits properly.
g   Red doesn't really look good on me. It isn't my color.
h   Which one do you like?

SALES CLERK   Hello—do you want any help?
ANDY   (1) _____
EMMA   Oh—look, Andy, these dresses are nice.
ANDY   (2) _____
EMMA   Only $45! That's really cheap.
ANDY   (3) _____
EMMA   The blue one.
ANDY   Great—so do I.
EMMA   (4) _____
SALES CLERK   Yes, sure. (5) _____

A few minutes later ...

EMMA   (6) _____
ANDY   No, it's too big.
EMMA   (7) _____
SALES CLERK   I don't think we have a smaller one in blue. What about this one?
EMMA   (8) _____
              I think I'll leave it.

3 Making requests

Rewrite the requests using *Would you mind ...ing?* and *Do you mind if I ...?*

1   Could you possibly drive me to the station?
    Would _____?
2   Can I please make a phone call?
    Do _____?
3   I wonder if you could turn the music down.
    Would _____?
4   Can I borrow your bike this afternoon?
    Do _____?
5   Could you set the table, please?
    Would _____?
6   Could I invite some friends over this evening?
    Do _____?

4 Vocabulary

Read and complete the dialogues with these words.

| change | double | evening | form | money | nights |
| passport | possible | receipt | reservation | shower |

In a bank

TOURIST   Could I (1) _____ 1,500 pesos into dollars?
TELLER   Yes—can I see your (2) _____?
TOURIST   Yes, of course.
TELLER   Thank you—how would you like the (3) _____?
TOURIST   In twenties, please.
TELLER   Here you go—and here's your (4) _____ for the exchange.
TOURIST   Thank you.

In a hotel

TOURIST   Good (5) _____—I'd like a room for two (6) _____, please.
DESK CLERK Have you made a (7) _____?
TOURIST   No, I haven't.
DESK CLERK That's no problem. Would you like a single or a (8) _____ room?
TOURIST   A single room, please, with a bath, if (9) _____.
DESK CLERK I'm sorry, we only have a single room with a (10) _____.
TOURIST   That's fine. I'll take it.
DESK CLERK Would you mind filling out this (11) _____, please?

5 Writing

A tourist at a train station wants to buy a single ticket to Boston. It's 2:30 and the next train leaves from platform 2 at 2:33. Complete the dialogue.

TOURIST   Can I (1) _____?
AGENT   One way (2) _____?
TOURIST   (3) _____
AGENT   That'll be $20.45—thank you. Here's your change.
TOURIST   When (4) _____?
AGENT   (5) _____ minutes.
TOURIST   Which (6) _____?
AGENT   (7) _____
TOURIST   (8) _____?
AGENT   No, it's a direct train.
TOURIST   (9) _____

61

6 ON THE MOVE

1 I promised I wouldn't forget!

1 Reading

Jake is traveling to South America and asked for travel tips on a website forum. Read the replies below, and complete the sentences using reported speech.

1 Sara told Jake _____
  Sara told him not _____

2 Dan explained _____

3 Ken advised him _____

4 Holly suggested _____

5 Max reminded him _____

6 Jenny warned him not _____

7 Kate said _____

> Pour liquids into plastic bottles—don't pack glass bottles.
> *Sara*

> It's best to drink lots of water during the flight so you'll feel less tired when you land.
> *Dan*

> Eat lots of garlic if you run out of insect spray because it will help to keep mosquitoes away.
> *Ken*

> If I were you, I'd cover your guidebook so you don't look like a tourist.
> *Holly*

> Remember to leave your room key at the hotel reception desk so you can't lose it.
> *Max*

> You shouldn't drink tap water or have ice in your drinks unless you're sure it's safe.
> *Jenny*

> I always take *Point It*—a little book of 1,200 pictures of things like food, drinks, etc. If you don't know the word for something, you can point to its picture!
> *Kate*

2 Reported speech

Match these sentences in reported speech with the pictures and write them in direct speech.

a Tom said he would have shrimp salad.
b Tom complained that the shrimp salad was too spicy.
c Sally replied that she'd love to.
d Sally suggested he drink some water.
e Sally suggested they sit by the window.
f ~~Tom invited Sally to have lunch in a restaurant.~~
g The waiter offered to bring him something else.
h Tom explained that he'd changed his mind.
i The waiter said they could sit where they liked.
j Sally pointed out that he didn't like seafood.

1 Would you like to have lunch in a restaurant?

62

UNIT 6

3 Reported speech

A group of tourists are on a package tour. Report what the speakers said using the verbs + (object) + infinitive.

1 JAMES Can I have a room with an ocean view? (ask)

James asked to have a room with an ocean view.

2 TOUR GUIDE Everyone should visit the old castle' (advise)

3 ANNA Peter, don't forget to change some money. (remind)

4 MIKE Janet, would you like to go to the pool? (invite)

5 KATHY Children, you can't spend too long on the beach. (warn)

6 CHILDREN We'll put on lots of sunscreen. (promise)

4 Reported speech

Report what the speakers said using the verbs in parentheses + (*that*) clause.

1 JAMES There aren't any towels in my room. (complain)

2 ANNA I hope it will stop raining soon. (hope)

3 KATHY Let's go on a boat trip. (suggest)

4 CHILDREN Yes, a boat trip will be fun. (agree)

5 JANET I'm feeling too tired to go swimming. (explain)

6 TOUR GUIDE No one should swim in the ocean when the red flag is up. (say)

5 Vocabulary

Match the verbs in list A with the words in list B.

	A	B
1	change	halfway around the world
2	take	your mind
3	come	pills
4	complain	someone to stay
5	invite	over this evening
6	travel	that something's wrong

6 Vocabulary

Match the words in list A with the words in list B and write eight compound nouns.

	A	B		
1	aisle	ache	**1**	*aisle seat*
2	grand	paper	**2**	
3	insect	board	**3**	
4	malaria	spray	**4**	
5	news	parents	**5**	
6	snow	seat	**6**	
7	tooth	pill	**7**	

7 Pronunciation

Circle the two rhyming words in each line.

1	(loud)	(crowd)	showed
2	aisle	fail	mile
3	towel	bowl	whole
4	seat	great	sheet
5	would	stood	food
6	ache	beach	wake
7	change	hang	strange
8	warn	earn	born

> **Extension** Write a postcard from Laura in India to a friend back home.

63

6

2 The waitress wanted to know if ...

ON THE MOVE

1 Reading

Read the text and complete it with these words.

accent   check-in   full   hard   hesitated   pardon   questions   sweetly   uncomfortably

Bryson Down Under

One of Bill Bryson's books, called **Down Under,** *is about Australia. This is a description of his arrival at a hotel in Uluru, which used to be known as Ayers Rock.*

Only one person, a man of about seventy, stood between me and the (1) .... desk of the very expensive Desert Gardens Hotel. All the other hotels in the town were (2) ....

"How big is it?" asked the man in an American (3) ....

"I beg your (4) .... ?" said the receptionist.

"How big is the room?"

The receptionist (5) .... "Well, I'm not sure exactly," he replied. "It's quite big."

"What does 'quite big' mean?" the American asked.

"Would you like to see the room?" the receptionist asked.

"No," the man said. "We want to get to the Rock."

But he then started asking a million other (6) .... "Where's the Rock?" "How long does it

take to get there?" "Is there a restaurant in the hotel?" "What time is dinner served?" "Can you see the Rock from the dining room?" "Where's the pool?" "Where's the elevator?"

I looked at my watch. I was (7) .... aware that it was two o'clock and I still didn't have a room.

Then the man's wife joined him and she began asking questions. "Is there a hairdresser's?" "How late does it open?" "Where can I send postcards?" "How much are stamps to the U.S.?" "Where's the gift shop?" "Does the gift shop take U.S. dollars?" "And what about my brain?" "Have you seen that anywhere?" (No, she didn't ask the last two questions—I made them up.)

Finally, they left, and the receptionist turned to me.

"Do you have a room, please?" I asked (8) ....

"No, sir," he replied. "I'm afraid that they," and he pointed to the man and his wife, "have just taken the last room."

I thought this was rather (9) .... on me. The nearest hotel was in Alice Springs, 500 kilometers away.

2 Reported questions

Write the questions in reported speech.

1 "How big is the room?" (ask)
The man *asked how big the room was.*

2 "What does 'quite big' mean?" (want to know)
He ....

3 "Would you like to see the room?" (wonder)
The receptionist ....

4 "Where's the Rock?" (ask)
The man ....

5 "How long does it take to get there?" (want to know)
He ....

6 "Is there a restaurant in the hotel?" (ask)
He ....

7 "What time is dinner served?" (want to know)
He ....

8 "Can you see the Rock from the dining room?" (ask)
He ....

9 "Is there a hairdresser's?" (ask)
The woman ....

10 "How late does it open?" (want to know)
She ....

11 "Where can I send postcards?" (ask)
She ....

12 "Where's the gift shop?" (ask)
She ....

13 "Does the gift shop take U.S. dollars?" (want to know)
She ....

14 "Do you have a room, please?" (wonder)
Bill ....

UNIT **6**

3 Reported speech

Match these answers with questions 1–14 in exercise 2.

1 The receptionist said that he wasn't sure whether it did or not. _13_

2 He offered to mail them from reception. ....

3 He said you could have your hair cut at any time during the day. ....

4 He offered to show the man the room. ....

5 He said that there were two. ....

6 He explained that the man and his wife had taken the last room. ....

7 He pointed out that you could see it from the gardens. ....

8 He said that it didn't take long. ....

9 He said that there was a hairdresser's. ....

10 The American refused the offer. ....

11 The receptionist explained where the gift shop was. ....

12 He said that he wasn't exactly sure, but that it was quite big. ....

13 He explained that it was served all evening. ....

14 He explained that it was not far from the hotel. ....

4 Reported questions

A travel writer tells a friend about a TV interview which she had. Write the questions in reported speech.

Interviewer	**Travel writer**
1 "Do you enjoy traveling?"	He asked _if I enjoyed traveling._
2 "Where would you like to go next?"	He wondered ....
3 "What's your favorite country?"	He wanted to know ....
4 "How many languages can you speak?"	He asked ....
5 "Do you take a laptop with you?"	He wanted to know ....
6 "Which book did you enjoy writing most?"	He asked ....
7 "Have you ever felt in danger?"	He wondered ....
8 "What should every traveler take with them?"	He asked ....
9 "When will your new book come out?"	He wanted to know ....
10 "Could you give some advice to a new writer?"	He asked ....

5 Vocabulary

Match the words in list A with the words in list B and write five compound nouns.

	A		B		
1	home		dressing	**1**	_homeland_
2	cash		water	**2**	....
3	paper		napkin	**3**	....
4	salad		register	**4**	....
5	ice		land	**5**	....

6 Vocabulary

Order the letters to find words to do with restaurants.

1 n r s d e s i g ....

2 r v g y a ....

3 s a t w s i r e ....

4 a n n k p i ....

5 a s c h e i r t g s r e ....

6 e t u k h p c ....

7 r y t a ....

7 Vocabulary

Match these words and phrases with their definitions.

> damp drown mainly starving wipe wrap

1 slightly wet ....

2 clean or dry something with a cloth ....

3 very hungry ....

4 sink underwater ....

5 put paper, etc. around something ....

6 mostly ....

8 Pronunciation

Write the number of syllables and mark the stress.

■
customer _3_ hesitate .... homeland ....

ketchup .... napkin .... rediscover ....

remark .... uncomfortably .... waitress ....

> **Extension** Write a paragraph about a memorable meal in a restaurant. What did you eat and drink? Who did you go with?

65

6 ON THE MOVE

3 You'd like to stay there, wouldn't you?

1 Reading

Read Sophie and Zak's conversation and complete it with tag questions.

ZAK   Is that another picture from the unusual buildings website?

SOPHIE   Yes, it is. You've seen some of these buildings before, (**1**) _____?

ZAK   Oh, I think I've seen a picture of that before. It's in Prague, (**2**) _____?

SOPHIE   Yes, that's right. It's called *The Dancing House*. It was designed by Frank Gehry.

ZAK   He's an American, (**3**) _____?

SOPHIE   Yes, he's from California. The house really looks as if it is dancing, (**4**) _____?

ZAK   Yes, it does. I think it's supposed to represent Fred Astaire and Ginger Rogers dancing.

SOPHIE   They were famous American movie stars, (**5**) _____?

ZAK   That's right.

SOPHIE   You've never been to Prague on vacation, (**6**) _____?

ZAK   No, never. I'd love to go.

2 Tag questions

Complete with these tag questions.

couldn't you   did he   did you   didn't I   didn't they   hasn't it   haven't we   isn't it   weren't they   would they

1 The buildings were all special in some way, _____?

2 Zak didn't understand why they chose those particular buildings, _____?

3 The Shanghai World Expo pavilion has been in the news recently, _____?

4 You could make the building change color by moving around in it, _____?

5 After the Expo was over, they recycled the building, _____?

6 The world's biggest igloo is in Canada, _____?

7 You didn't know that the world's tallest skyscraper was in Dubai, _____?

8 They wouldn't let Zak into the world's most expensive hotel, _____?

9 We've seen that picture before, _____?

10 I asked you to bring the camera, _____?

3 Tag questions

Complete with tag questions.

1 The buildings were on the website, ...?
2 The buildings had all been chosen because they were special, ...?
3 Zak didn't understand what the website was about, ...?
4 Sophie had to explain things to Zak, ...?
5 You can't visit the exhibition pavilion from the Shanghai World Expo, ...?
6 The world's tallest skyscraper is in Dubai, ...?
7 They hadn't visited the art museum in Vienna, ...?
8 They'd been looking at the pictures, ...?
9 Sophie would like to stay in the Governor Villa, ...?
10 You've stayed in an ice hotel, ...?

4 Vocabulary

Match the words and phrases in list A with the words and phrases in list B.

	A	B
1	expect someone	color
2	let	out of something
3	be in	a lot of people
4	stay	someone in
5	cost a lot	to know something
6	hold	the news
7	make something	in a hotel
8	change	of money

5 Vocabulary

Match the words in list A with the words in list B and write six compound words.

	A	B		
1	boy	down	1	*boyfriend*
2	sky	friend	2	
3	hotel	museum	3	
4	upside	site	4	
5	art	room	5	
6	web	scraper	6	

6 Crossword

Complete the crossword puzzle and find the extra word ↓.

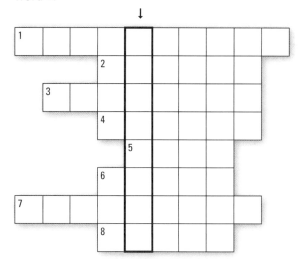

1 The pavilion in Shanghai was built for an …
2 The modern art … is in Vienna.
3 Frank Gehry … *The Dancing House* in Prague.
4 The Dubai skyscraper has 160 …
5 The house on the roof of the art museum is upside …
6 It costs $7,200 a … to stay in the Governor Villa.
7 The Governor Villa is a very … hotel suite.
8 This building is made of ice.

7 Pronunciation

Write the number of syllables and mark the stress.

exhibition *4*   expensive ......   igloo ......
pavilion ......   skyscraper ......   unusual ......

> **Extension** Write a paragraph about your favorite building or an unusual building you know.

6 ON THE MOVE

4 Integrated Skills

Reporting and summarizing what people said

1 Reading

Read *Traveling with parents*. Then complete the text with ten of the phrases a–l. There are two extra phrases.

a we go on fishing expeditions
b with a schoolfriend and her parents
c and you feel that your vacation has really begun
d I love walking
e and our guide had a surprise cake for her
f but sometimes they come here to Washington, D.C.
g like necklaces out of shells
h so we do a different section each summer
i which are really cramped
j It's time we went somewhere else
k if you stop for a rest and to see things along the way
l sit around the swimming pool

Traveling with parents

Sayuri Nakahama, 17, is a student in Washington, D.C.

Do you go on vacation with your parents?
My parents live in California but my brother and I are at school in Washington, D.C. During vacations we sometimes fly back to California to stay with Mom and Dad, (**1**) _____ and then we go on vacation together. But this year, we are walking part of the Appalachian Trail in Virginia. The whole walk is almost 3,500 kilometers long, (**2**) _____. We have a long way to go before we finish the whole trail. Our parents like hiking a lot, and we have also been on hiking vacations in Colorado and California. Last Christmas, we climbed a mountain in Yosemite National Park in California. There were birds, deer, and lizards everywhere. It was amazing. It was my mom's birthday the day we went to the top, (**3**) _____. He had carried it all the way up the mountain!

What do you like doing most on vacation?
(**4**) _____, of course. But I also have vacations with my family in Japan which don't involve much exercise. That's where my grandparents live, and we'll (**5**) _____ and have picnics on the beach. When I was little, I loved visiting my grandmother. She's really good at cooking and making things (**6**) _____.

What's your favorite means of travel?
Ferries. There's plenty of space, not like cars and planes, (**7**) _____. And you can walk around on deck and enjoy the fresh air. I love that moment when you first see the coastline that the ferry is heading towards—it's so exciting (**8**) _____.

What are your tips for family vacations?
Have more breaks on long trips. Parents don't realize that traveling is part of the vacation too, and everyone will be in a better mood for the next part of the trip (**9**) _____.

Where are you going on your next vacation?
To North Carolina, staying in a house (**10**) _____. It's on an island, and there are great beaches there. It's exciting to be going on vacation with a friend. I still like family vacations, though, and I'm looking forward to seeing my parents in the summer and doing the last part of our walk together.

68

2 Vocabulary

Find words in *Traveling with parents* on page 68 that mean the same as these phrases.

1 path or track through the countryside

2 the hard covering of a sea creature

3 opposite of *spacious*

4 small reptile with a long tail

5 way someone feels

6 outside top floor of a boat

3 Crossword

Complete the crossword puzzle.

Across →

1 ... can protect you against diseases. (12)
7 The simple past of *come*. (4)
8 Do you have any ...s for the weekend? (4)
9 You'd like ... stay there, wouldn't you? (2)
10 I don't mind soccer. It's ... (2)
12 The opposite of *short*. (4)
13 It's the biggest museum ... the world. (2)
15 When you eat, you use a knife and ... (4)
16 I don't want to wait. Let's go ...! (3)
18 This round, white vegetable has a strong smell. (5)
20 The fourth month. (5)
21 I haven't travelled ... much as you. (2)
22 I'm sorry, I don't speak Spanish. I don't ... (9)

Down ↓

1 Do you go on ... with your parents? (8)
2 Laura had an Indian meal, and ... it was too spicy. (10)
3 This protects your clothes when you're eating. (6)
4 Don't take more clothes ... you need. (4)
5 This bag isn't small enough to take ... the plane. (2)
6 You can see fish underwater when you go ... (10)
11 Laura's parents were ... about the trip to India. They wanted to meet Nisha's parents first. (7)
14 Say: "..., thank you" to refuse something politely. (2)
17 When ... your last vacation? (3)
19 MoMA is very ... Central Park in New York City. (4)
21 MoMA is the Museum of Modern ... (3)

UNIT 6

LEARNER INDEPENDENCE

Predicting and listening

You can improve your listening skills by listening to the news. You can hear the news in English on the CNN website and on the websites of many other broadcasters.

Before listening, prepare yourself by:

- looking at today's news in your own language in a newspaper or online
- listening to the news in your own language on the radio or online
- making notes of the main topics of international news
- reading today's news in English in a newspaper or online
- writing down the key words in English and checking their meaning in a dictionary

Then listen to the news in English once for general understanding. Listen a second time and write down the topics of the main news stories. Listen a third time and write notes under each topic. Finally, listen again and check your notes.

Extensive reading

Read an English story and write a 50-word summary of the story.

69

6 ON THE MOVE

Inspired EXTRA!

CONSOLIDATION

LESSON 1

Write the sentences in reported speech using the verbs in parentheses.

1 "Can you help me?" (ask)

He *asked me to help him.*

2 "Yes, I'll help you." (agree)

I

3 "Listen carefully." (tell)

He

4 "Should I take notes?" (offer)

I

5 "Don't tell anyone about it." (warn)

He

6 "Of course I won't tell anyone." (promise)

I

LESSON 2

Tim has just moved to a new town. Report his questions using the verbs in parentheses.

1 "How many people live in the town?" (want to know)

He wanted to know how many people lived in the town.

2 "Where's the nearest movie theater?" (ask)

3 "Is there somewhere I can play basketball?" (wonder)

4 "Do you need any ID to get into the clubs?" (want to know)

5 "When is the last bus in the evening?" (ask)

6 "Which is the best soccer team to support?" (want to know)

7 "Are there lots of things to do in the evening?" (wonder)

8 "Does it take a long time to walk to school?" (ask)

LESSON 3

Complete the tag questions.

1 The weather is great today, *isn't it* ?

2 You're not from the U.S., ?

3 Those were expensive boots, ?

4 He doesn't like modern art, ?

5 You can't come to the meeting tonight, ?

6 She'd like to visit us here, ?

7 They didn't get our message, ?

8 This building holds 10,000 people, ?

LESSON 4

Write questions for these answers about *Family Vacations* on page 80 of the Student's Book.

1 *How long did it take to fly from Toronto to Buenos Aires?*

13 hours.

2

A traditional Andean stew.

3

Spanish.

4

Mendoza.

5

Because Isabel wanted a beach vacation.

Spelling

Correct the spelling of these words from Unit 6 by doubling one letter in each word.

1 dresing 2 iglo 3 lugage 4 oposite 5 originaly

6 rol 7 shoping 8 sightseing 9 sugest

10 swetly 11 vacination 12 waitres

Brainteaser

What's the longest word in the English language?

Answer on page 73.

70

UNIT 6

EXTENSION

LESSON 1

Report what the speakers said using these verbs.

> agree   complain   explain   promise   remind   suggest

1 LAURA   Nisha, don't forget to come to dinner tonight.
Laura reminded Nisha to come to dinner tonight.

2 NISHA   You keep telling me not to forget things.

3 LAURA   I'm sorry, Nisha. I won't do it again.

4 NISHA   I'm upset because my father is angry with me.

5 LAURA   Why don't you talk to your father about the problem?

6 NISHA   Yes. That's a good idea.

LESSON 2

Greg is flying alone for the first time. Report his questions for these answers.

1 Greg asked   *when he had to check in.*
"You have to check in at least two hours before take-off."

2 He wanted to know
"Yes, that's enough time to go through security."

3 He wondered
"Yes, you can choose your seat when you check in."

4 He wanted to know
"No, you can't use a cell phone on the plane."

5 He wondered
"Yes, you are allowed to take pictures with a camera but not with a phone."

6 He asked
"Yes, you can have a vegetarian meal if you tell the airline in advance."

LESSON 3

Complete the tag questions with your own ideas.

1 You _____, don't you?
2 Your parents _____, do they?
3 The weather today _____, isn't it?
4 You'd like to _____, wouldn't you?
5 You've never _____, have you?
6 You can't _____, can you?
7 Yesterday, your friends _____, didn't they?
8 You _____, did you?

LESSON 4

Look at exercise 5 on page 81 of the Student's Book and use your notes to write a summary of what Ben said in the interview. Use reported speech.

Web watch

Work with a partner and plan a trip to the United States. Go to *visitusa.com* and click on the state you want to visit.

Spelling

Write the homophones of these words. All the homophones are in Unit 6.

1 /aɪl/ I'll
2 /raɪt/ write
3 /ræp/ rap
4 /sin/ scene
5 /baɪ/ by
6 /wɔrn/ worn

Brainteaser

What should you keep because no one else wants it?

Answer on page 73.

71

REVIEW

UNITS 5–6

1 Read the text. For each number 1–15, choose word or phrase A, B, C, or D.

Extreme wheelchair adventures

Just because someone has to use a wheelchair doesn't mean that they can't try (**1**) _____ and exciting activities.

Piers Stone (**2**) _____ to cycle 400 kilometers through Kenya for five days with a group of other disabled cyclists to raise money for charity. Piers uses a special wheelchair and cycles using his hands. He (**3**) _____ that the cyclists woke at 5:30 every morning and sometimes (**4**) _____ bike all day to reach their next stop. He was helped by his friend, Sylwia Borek. "I couldn't (**5**) _____ this crazy challenge without her," said Piers. His trip has raised over $6,000 for charity.

Gordon Rattray was a tour guide in Africa before he broke his neck in Mali in 1998. After his accident, he returned to Africa, where he got to (**6**) _____ an elephant (**7**) _____ well! "There wasn't a sound," said Gordon, "just the noise of the elephant's huge feet in the dry grass. He walked slowly straight up to our little brown car and looked down his trunk at me. I was terrified. Being a wheelchair user made no (**8**) _____ in this situation. I'd (**9**) _____ too scared to run away, even if I had been able to! The elephant stood next to us—I'd have been able to touch him if I (**10**) _____ to—for at least five minutes. Then he calmly raised his trunk, smelled the air, and decided to walk on. I began to breathe again. Moments like this make all the hard work of travel in Africa worth it, (**11**) _____?"

For other people, it's the cold rather than the heat which is attractive, and more and more wheelchair users are learning to ski. "I wish I (**12**) _____ about this before," one said. "You can't (**13**) _____ it. I love being independent and I wanted to know if I could ski (**14**) _____. After a couple of days' practice the instructor told me that I (**15**) _____ as daring as I liked." Wheelchair skiers have special equipment made for them, and can attempt even the most difficult ski runs.

1 A dangerous	**B** infectious	**C** nervous	**D** spacious
2 A advised	**B** offered	**C** refused	**D** warned
3 A agreed	**B** explained	**C** promised	**D** suggested
4 A need	**B** have to	**C** needed	**D** had to
5 A do	**B** doing	**C** done	**D** have done
6 A be	**B** have	**C** know	**D** look
7 A exactly	**B** responsibly	**C** regularly	**D** uncomfortably
8 A change	**B** exchange	**C** difference	**D** different
9 A be	**B** been	**C** have been	**D** had been
10 A 've wanted	**B** 'd wanted	**C** wanted	**D** was wanting
11 A do they	**B** doesn't it	**C** don't they	**D** aren't they
12 A 've heard	**B** 'd heard	**C** heard	**D** was hearing
13 A beat	**B** eat	**C** heat	**D** meet
14 A among	**B** mainly	**C** solo	**D** together
15 A be	**B** being	**C** can be	**D** could be

2 Complete with the correct form of the words in capitals.

1 The *Titanic* was said to be _____ .   SINK

2 The file contains all the _____ of the model.   MEASURE

3 There were 200 _____ after the accident.   SURVIVE

4 Maribel Dominguez is talented and _____ .   COURAGE

5 You can't get a _____ against malaria yet.   VACCINE

6 He was very happy to _____ his old friends.   DISCOVER

7 Congratulations! You're the _____ student in the class.   BEHAVE

8 It's a popular song—it's really _____ .   KNOW

3 Complete the second sentence so that it means the same as the first sentence.

1 He didn't buy the laptop because he didn't have enough money. If _____

2 Now she regrets that she didn't ask for some advice. She wishes _____

3 You aren't allowed to dive on your own. You can't _____

4 I'm sure that they left the party before I arrived. They must _____

5 My mother said that it would be a good idea to invite them. My mother suggested _____

6 Laura said that she would call every day. Laura promised _____

7 "Laura, what do you feel like doing tonight?" asked Nisha. Nisha asked Laura _____

8 It's warm, isn't it? It isn't cold, _____

4 Find the word that is different.

1 abduct   arrest   catch   avoid

2 voyage   message   flight   trip

3 ship   boat   tank   yacht

4 survive   drown   die   freeze

5 author   customer   flower   navigator

6 sarong   sheet   pill   towel

7 best-behaved   hand-carved   short-haired   well-dressed

8 reappear   remark   remember   remind

Answers to Brainteasers

UNIT 5
Consolidation Are you asleep?
Extension The letter *e*.

UNIT 6
Consolidation "Smiles"—there's a mile between the first *s* and the last *s*.
Extension Your temper.

LEARNER INDEPENDENCE
SELF ASSESSMENT

Vocabulary

1 Draw this chart in your notebook. How many words can you write in each category?

More than 10? Good!   *More than 12?* Very good!
More than 15? Excellent!

Aviation	
Restaurants	
Travel and vacations	

2 Put the words in order to make expressions from the phrasebooks in Lesson 4 in Units 1 and 2.

1 why don't know I
I don't know why.

2 words in other …

3 chance the wanted just I given be to

4 happened have could what

5 my I've mind changed

6 guess you'll never what …

7 question it's of out the

8 fact opposite the was in it

Check your answers.
8/8 Excellent!   *6/8* Very good!   *4/8* Try again!

My learning diary
In Units 5 and 6:
My favorite topic is _____

My favorite picture is _____

The three lessons I like most are _____

My favorite activity or exercise is _____

Something I don't understand is _____

Something I want to learn more about is _____

73

7 GETTING THE MESSAGE ACROSS

1 Good job—keep it up!

1 Reading

Read the text and complete it with these words.

been	described	experiments	explain	expression
have	origin	suggested	tested	used	will	written

What does it mean?

Everyone knows that "You're pulling my leg" means "You're kidding," but no one knows where the expression comes from! It's thought that it was first said in the nineteenth century, but it may be older. It's been (**1**) _____ that it refers to the way a street thief might kick someone's leg to make them fall over. But this doesn't (**2**) _____ why we say "pulling."

The idiom "in the red" is easier. In the past, bank statements were (**3**) _____ in black when you had money in the bank, and in red when you'd taken more money out of the bank than was available. So if a company is losing money, it's (**4**) _____ as being "in the red."

Many explanations have (**5**) _____ offered for the (**6**) _____ of the expression "knock on wood." It's used to keep away bad luck, e.g., "I think I've passed the exam—knock on wood." It's been argued that it's an Irish (**7**) _____ to do with knocking on or touching special trees. Other experts (**8**) _____ claimed that it's to do with touching the Christian cross or knocking on a church door. These suggestions make it seem very old, but in fact it was first used only a hundred years ago. In the U.K. they say "Touch wood," and this (**9**) _____ also be understood if it is said in the U.S.

The expression "to be a guinea pig" is thought to come from the use of these animals in medical and scientific (**10**) _____. Why the animal itself is called a guinea pig is a mystery, as it is neither a pig nor from Guinea! Guinea pigs come from South America and were first (**11**) _____ by Pasteur in his work at the end of the nineteenth century. The first use of the expression to describe something being (**12**) _____ on a human is dated 1913.

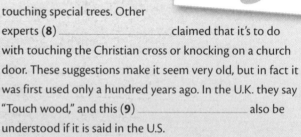

2 Simple present and present progressive passive

Complete with the simple present or present progressive passive of the verbs.

New words are invented every day—in fact new words (**1**) _____ (invent) while you're doing this exercise! The way in which words are being used is also changing. For example, "I'm good" (**2**) _____ (use) by some people in reply to the question "How are you?", rather than "I'm fine." So the language (**3**) _____ constantly _____ (change) as new words and new ways of using old words are created. People aren't always sure what (**4**) _____ (mean) by some of the new expressions. It's therefore important that dictionaries are revised to keep up with all the new words and expressions that (**5**) _____ (create) all the time.

3 Present perfect passive

Changing People is a TV show where a person's appearance is changed in a day. Write sentences about Tim using the present perfect passive of the verbs.

1 his hair/cut/and/wash
   _____

2 his shoes/clean
   _____

3 his nails/cut
   _____

4 new clothes/buy for him
   _____

5 everything/pay for by the TV company
   _____

TIM

BEFORE   AFTER

UNIT 7

4 Passive tenses

Complete using the correct passive form of the verbs in parentheses.

Communication Problems

Although e-mail (**1**) _____ (use/*present progressive*) more and more to send messages, a number of problems (**2**) _____ (create/*present perfect*) by its success. In the past, messages (**3**) _____ (send/*simple past*) in letters, and people were accustomed to waiting for a reply. But now with e-mail you (**4**) _____ (expect/*simple present*) to reply at once. Another problem (**5**) _____ (cause/*present perfect*) by the ease and economy with which e-mail (**6**) _____ (transmit/*simple present*) and everyone (**7**) _____ (affect/*simple present*) by it—spam. No one doubts that the problem of spam (**8**) _____ (solve/*future simple*) but the question is—when? Everyone receives some junk mail through the mail but at least you (**9**) _____ (not expect/*simple present*) to read it more than once a day. Spam (**10**) _____ (sent/*simple present*) all the time so you get it every time you check your e-mail. In offices, phone conversations (**11**) _____ (replace/*present progressive*) by e-mail, so people in the same building don't often speak to each other. In the future, more and more workers (**12**) _____ (forbid/ *simple future*) to use e-mail for part of the day so that they can have more interaction with each other.

5 Vocabulary

Match the verbs in list A with the words and phrases in list B. Then write the phrases.

	A	B		
1	hang	a wall	**1**	*hang a blind*
2	install	an ankle	**2**	
3	repaint	a new stove	**3**	
4	send	a blind	**4**	
5	twist	a chain e-mail	**5**	

6 Vocabulary

Compare the words in list A with the words in list B. Write *S* if they have almost the same meaning, *O* if they are opposites, and *G* if A is more general than B.

	A	B	
1	jumbo-sized	tiny	*O*
2	constantly	regularly	
3	game	badminton	
4	kitchen equipment	stove	
5	injure	hurt	
6	put up	remove	
7	furniture	cupboard	
8	prize	award	

7 Vocabulary

Match these idioms with their definitions.

> be fired   be under the weather   jumbo
> keep it up   know the ropes   wicked (*slang*)

1	not feel very well	
2	very big	
3	understand what to do	
4	lose a job	
5	very good	
6	continue doing well	

8 Pronunciation

Write the number of syllables and mark the stress.

■
constantly _3_   demonstration _____   encourage _____

experience _____   expression _____   furniture _____

idiomatic _____   nautical _____   repaint _____   unusually _____

Extension Think of an idiom in your language. Write a paragraph explaining what it means, and where you think the expression comes from.

7 GETTING THE MESSAGE ACROSS

2 She deserves to be awarded a prize

1 Reading

Read this summary of the *United Nations Declaration of the Rights of the Child (1959)* and complete it with the correct form of the verbs.

> allow   give   make   offer   protect   provide   teach

All children have these rights, whatever their race, color, sex, language, religion, political, or other opinion, wherever they were born, and whoever they were born to.

- You should (1) _____ to grow up and to develop physically and mentally in a healthy and normal way.
- You have the right to a name and to be a citizen of a country.
- You must be (2) _____ and (3) _____ with good food, housing, and medical services.
- You have the right to special care if you are disabled in any way.
- You should (4) _____ love and understanding, by parents and family if they can, or by the government if they cannot give them.
- You have the right to go to school free, to play, and to learn to be responsible and useful.
- You must always be the first to (5) _____ help when needed.
- You shouldn't (6) _____ to work before you are old enough, or do other things which could damage your health or development.
- You should (7) _____ to value peace, understanding, and friendship between people of all countries.

2 Passive infinitive

Complete with the passive infinitive.

According to Dr. Lynne Elkin of California State University, even James Watson agrees that Rosalind Franklin should (1) _____ (award) the Nobel Prize for her work on DNA. But she can't (2) _____ (give) it because she is no longer alive, and dead people are not allowed (3) _____ (honor) in this way. Dr. Elkin says it must (4) _____ (understand) that Franklin was close to discovering the structure of DNA. It ought (5) _____ (remember) that without Photo 51, Crick and Watson could not have made their discovery. And it should (6) _____ (point out) that if they had read an article by Franklin about Photo 51, they would have had to acknowledge her work. But because Maurice Wilkins showed Watson the photo secretly, they decided that Franklin did not have (7) _____ (acknowledge). Dr. Elkin thinks that Franklin's contribution must (8) _____ (recognize) and she has suggested that the structure which was discovered should (9) _____ (call) the Watson-Crick-Franklin structure. Dr. Elkin believes that Photo 51 ought (10) _____ (give) its correct place in the history of science.

3 Passive infinitive

Complete with the passive infinitive of these verbs.

> allow   do   give   obey   show

Dr. Catherine Walter of the University of Oxford has this advice for her students about acknowledging quotes in essays and why this has (1) ....

Communities, for example, the people who play tennis all over the world, the participants in an online role-playing game, or the people who usually go to a particular coffee shop on Tuesday evening, all have rules. Some rules may be written; others are unwritten. Some rules are more important than others. But they all must (2) .... It isn't necessarily morally wrong, and it isn't always against the law, for a member to break a rule of the community. However, breaking a rule has consequences; and seriously breaking an important rule can mean that a member can't (3) .... to continue as a member of a community.

When we borrow from someone else's work when writing an essay, for example, an acknowledgement must (4) .... of who we are quoting from. Then the reader can know what part of what we have written is our own work. It is a rule of the educational community that the sources of quotes must always be listed. Sources must (5) .... because if they aren't, it makes it seem that someone else's words are actually your own.

4 *either ... or, both ... and*

Complete with *either ... or* or *both ... and*.

1 Teenagers can be treated .... as adults .... as children, but not as both at the same time.
2 It's not often that .... father .... mother agree on how to treat teenage children.
3 .... teenagers .... adults should be encouraged to do as much exercise as possible.
4 Parents and teachers can .... listen to the views of teenagers .... deal with the consequences if they don't.
5 It's simple: .... trust your children .... lose them.

5 Crossword

Complete the crossword puzzle and find the extra word ↓.

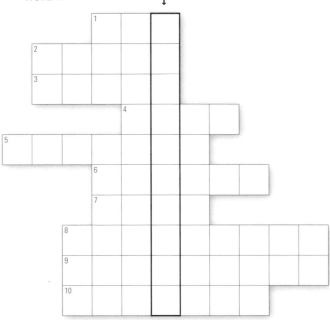

1 A chemical. Everyone's ... is different.
2 Jocelyn Bell Burnell discovered tiny ... called pulsars.
3 Bright object in space which has a tail of gas.
4 Rosalind Franklin took ... pictures of atoms.
5 Nuclear ... is the process of dividing an atom.
6 Rosalind Franklin died of this disease.
7 Photo 51 was a picture of an ...
8 Otto Hahn won the Nobel Prize for ...
9 The Franklin prize is given to a woman ...
10 The Nobel Prize was ... to Crick and Watson.

6 Vocabulary

Match the verbs in list A with the words and phrases in list B. Then write the phrases.

A	B	
1 award	a mystery	1 *award a prize*
2 be put	from something	2 ....
3 benefit	in one's place	3 ....
4 change	a prize	4 ....
5 solve	the rules	5 ....

7 Pronunciation

Write the number of syllables and mark the stress.

astronomer *4*   brilliant ......   chemistry ......

comet ......   deserve ......   ironically ......   nuclear ......

persuade ......   prejudice ......   recognized ......

> **Extension** Write a paragraph about someone you know who deserves to be awarded a prize. What has this person done and why do you think he or she should get a prize?

7 GETTING THE MESSAGE ACROSS

3 They couldn't call up a doctor

A lifeline for Africa

The increase in cell phone use in Africa doesn't just mean that it is easier for people to stay in touch with friends and relatives.

It has also opened up business opportunities, particularly for people in remote areas of the country. Now fisherman can find out by phone from market traders what kind of fish the shoppers in the markets are asking for. The fishermen can then go out in their boats, catch the right fish, deliver them to the markets, and make the most profit.

In some of the poorer communities, phone sharing—having one cell phone, which can be used by several people who all share the cost—is becoming more common. It has encouraged the growth of many small businesses which are run by people who could never afford the phone charges on their own.

The cell phone is also transforming medical care. Health workers in small rural medical centers can use their cell phones to order medicine, ask for advice on the treatment of their patients, and report on a patient's progress to doctors in larger, better-equipped hospitals in the cities. They are also benefiting from the fact that the latest phones can be used for much more than just making phone calls. Phones have now been developed that can be used to measure a patient's heart and breathing rate, take their temperature, and record other vital signs. This can all be done thousands of miles from a hospital or medical center, and the data can be sent through so that a doctor can give the best advice about how the patient should be treated. While many of these phones were developed for people in rich countries, for people in developing countries, they can be a real life-saver.

1 Reading

Read the text. Then read the sentences and write *T* (true) or *F* (false).

1 People in Africa don't use their phones for social and family contact. ☐

2 Fishermen can make more profit if they catch the right kind of fish. ☐

3 In phone sharing, one person who can afford a phone allows other people to use it. ☐

4 Health workers in Africa sometimes call doctors to ask for advice about how to treat patients. ☐

5 Cell phones which can measure things like temperature were developed specifically for people in developing countries. ☐

2 Verb + preposition with direct object

Rewrite the sentences replacing the words in *italics* with pronouns.

1 She wrote down *the message*.

2 He looked up *the number* in his address book

3 He held up *his cell phone*.

4 She wanted to speak to *her friends*.

5 I hung up *the phone* when I had finished.

6 He remembered to turn on *his phone*.

7 She climbed up *the stairs*.

8 She spoke with *her parents* for an hour.

3 Vocabulary

Read the sentences and replace the words in *italics* using the correct form of these phrasal verbs.

> call back   come down   find out   go on
> go up   hold on   pick up   put through

1. The office manager asked the caller to *try again* in an hour.
2. The price of computers is *falling* all the time.
3. I can never *receive* a cell phone signal in my apartment.
4. The extension was busy so I had to *wait on the telephone* until someone answered.
5. I *discovered* her phone number by asking her friend.
6. The number of teenagers with cell phones *increased* even more last year.
7. Please *continue*—it's very interesting.
8. The receptionist *connected* the caller to the right department.

4 Crossword

Complete the crossword puzzle and find the extra word ↓.

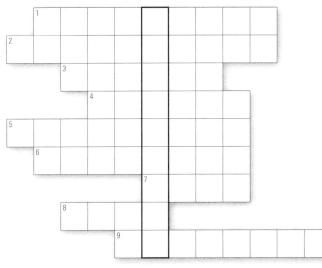

1. Very many; too many to count.
2. Person who pays for a phone service.
3. Ten years.
4. Seller.
5. A very large increase in something over a short time.
6. A raised, flat surface.
7. Spoken.
8. Someone who uses something.
9. Special importance given to something.

5 Vocabulary

Number the sentences to show the order of this telephone conversation.

- OK, I'll give her your message as soon as possible. ....
- Yes, that would be fine. ....
- Yes, of course. What's the message? ....
- I'd like to speak to the manager, please. ....
- I see. Can I leave a message then? ....
- Please call Helen at 555-7833. ....
- I'm sorry, I'm afraid his line's busy, too. ....
- Oh, sorry, the line's busy. Would you like to speak to her assistant? ....
- Thank you very much. Goodbye. ....
- Good afternoon, can I help you? ....

6 Vocabulary

Complete with these words and phrases.

> a bus   a deal   up a ladder   up a signal
> up a doctor   out the answer

1. call   ....
2. climb   ....
3. find   ....
4. make   ....
5. pick   ....
6. take   ....

7 Vocabulary

Match the words in list A with the words in list B and write six compound nouns.

A	B	
1 bus	address	1 *bus conductor*
2 e-mail	conductor	2
3 host	telling	3
4 landline	vendor	4
5 story	family	5
6 street	subscriber	6

8 Pronunciation

Write the number of syllables and mark the stress.

conductor *3*   communicate ....   decade ....

emphasis ....   entrepreneur ....   landline ....

platform ....   revolution ....   sociologist ....

subscriber ....   transform ....

> **Extension** Write a new phone conversation similar to the one in exercise 5 and practice it with another student.

79

7 GETTING THE MESSAGE ACROSS

4 Integrated Skills
Discussing languages

1 Reading

Read *Welcome to Esperanto!* and complete the text with these words.

based   benefit   broadcast   communication   estimated   invented   magazines
official   produce   pronounced   published   regularly   simple   speakers   tenses

Welcome to Esperanto!

Many people believe that international communication would (1) .... greatly if more people used an "artificial" language (AL)—a language that has been specially (2) .... Several hundred ALs have been recorded, and new ones continue to be created. But the best-known AL is Esperanto, which was invented by Ludwig Lazarus Zamenhof.

Zamenhof, who was a Polish eye doctor, published his new "international language" in 1887 under the name Doktoro Esperanto ("Doctor Hopeful"), and "Esperanto" eventually became its (3) .... title. The first Universal Congress of Esperanto, which brought together nearly 700 people from 20 countries, was held in 1905. In the same year, *Fundamento de Esperanto* was (4) ...., a statement of the grammar and vocabulary of the language.

Esperanto, whose alphabet has five vowels and 20 consonants, is largely (5) .... on West European vocabulary, and its grammar is (6) .... All its nouns end in -o and plurals add -j. All adjectives which end in -a agree with the noun. There are present, past, and future (7) ...., and verbs have the same ending throughout a tense form. Compound words can be formed by combining word roots to (8) .... a large vocabulary, and great use is made of prefixes and suffixes. Every word in Esperanto is (9) .... exactly as it is spelled, and there are no silent letters.

Esperanto was designed to be an international second language, which people from different countries could learn easily and use to communicate. Today it is (10) .... that Esperanto has about two million (11) ...., and more than a hundred international conferences and meetings are held each year in the language. Thousands of books and dozens of newspapers and (12) .... are published in Esperanto, several countries (13) .... transmit Esperanto radio shows, and TV stations (14) .... Esperanto courses. And, these days, the Internet is the fastest-growing means of (15) .... among Esperanto speakers.

Finally, a frequently-asked question: how do you say "I love you" in Esperanto? The answer is: "Mi amas vin!"

2 Non-defining relative clauses

Find five non-defining relative clauses in *Welcome to Esperanto!* and underline them.

3 Non-defining relative clauses

Join the sentences using *which*, *who*, or *whose* in non-defining relative clauses. Don't forget to add commas!

1 The Cambodian alphabet is the world's largest alphabet. It has 74 letters.

2 The world's shortest alphabet has only 11 letters. It is used in the Solomon Islands.

3 The Berbers hardly ever write in their language. They live in North Africa.

4 Basque is not apparently related to any other language. It is spoken in northwest Spain and southwest France.

5 The Japanese have four writing systems: *kanji* (adapted from Chinese), *hiragana*, *katakana*, and *romaji*. Their language is difficult to learn.

4 Crossword

Complete the crossword puzzle.

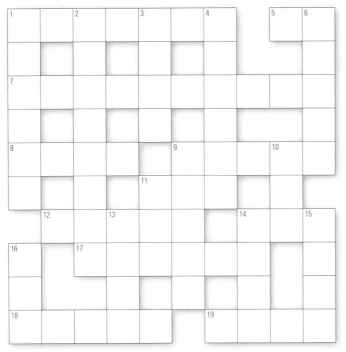

Across →

1. Books are usually kept on … (7)
5. You can use your dictionary to look … new words. (2)
7. Something that can't be done is … (10)
8. Very good, or opposite of *warm*. (4)
9. Places where people go swimming. (5)
11. Neither Franklin … Meitner was awarded a Nobel Prize. (3)
12. Opposite of *above*. (5)
14. No one had a cell phone 50 years … (3)
17. When you repeat a story, you … it. (6)
18. If you … your ankle, it's painful to walk. (5)
19. Soccer players hope to score this. (4)

Down ↓

1. Please turn on the light. The light … is on the wall over there. (5)
2. Someone who gives people work. (8)
3. You sometimes need a … when traveling abroad. (4)
4. Person who works on a boat. (6)
6. I have to … two keys to lock my cell phone. (5)
9. A cell phone gets … from its battery. (5)
10. Your ankle is at the bottom of your … (3)
11. *forbid* = … allow (3)
13. Some people think we should use e-mail … and talk to each other more. (4)
14. She speaks not only English, French, and Spanish, but … Chinese. (4)
15. To do with speaking. (4)
16. Kind of plane. (3)

UNIT 7

LEARNER INDEPENDENCE

Spelling and pronunciation

Unlike Esperanto, English words are often not pronounced as they are written, and the same series of letters may be pronounced differently in different words. For example, "ough" is pronounced differently in *though, through, thought, cough,* etc.

Try making charts of words with the same sound but different spellings. Add as many words as you can to this chart.

/aɪ/ as in *why*

y	*sky*
uy	*buy*
ie	*die*
igh	*high*

What other spellings of /ɔr/ do you know?

Extensive reading

Read an English book and write a review of the story for other students.

7 GETTING THE MESSAGE ACROSS

Inspired EXTRA!

CONSOLIDATION

LESSON 1

Complete with the simple past, present progressive, or simple future passive of the verbs.

1 The house _____ (repaint) last year.

2 The kitchen _____ (clean) now.

3 The new sink _____ (install) next week.

4 You can't use the car—it _____ (repair) right now.

5 The room _____ (prepare) before the guests arrived.

6 You _____ (expect) to help your mother tomorrow.

7 Your dinner _____ (cook) now.

8 The TV _____ (replace) when we have enough money.

LESSON 2

Complete with the passive infinitive of the verbs.

1 I don't think he can _____ (persuade) to come with us.

2 He doesn't deserve _____ (thank)— he hasn't done anything.

3 It ought _____ (forbid) to use a cell phone when riding a bike.

4 Her important work ought _____ (acknowledge).

5 They're very lazy—they must _____ (tell) to try harder.

6 She's beginning _____ (recognize) as an important artist.

7 I should _____ (give) more help. I can't do everything on my own.

8 The law should _____ (change) so that you can vote at 16.

LESSON 3

Rewrite the sentences, replacing the words in *italics* with pronouns and the underlined verbs with the correct form of these phrasal verbs.

> come down   find out   pick up   put up   call up

1 Remember to <u>telephone</u> *your sister* when you arrive.

_____

2 He said *the price of international calls* was <u>falling</u>.

_____

3 My cell phone couldn't <u>receive</u> *a signal* in the kitchen.

_____

4 I couldn't <u>discover</u> *her number*.

_____

5 Are they allowed to <u>build</u> *cell phone towers* near schools?

_____

LESSON 4

Match these words with their definitions.

1	a half dozen	a	six
2	extinction	b	more and more
3	increasingly	c	word or phrase
4	murder	d	set of plans agreed by, e.g. a government or company
5	policy		
6	term	e	when someone is killed, not by chance or accident
		f	when an animal, plant, or language no longer exists

Spelling

Fill in the silent letters of these words from Unit 7.

1 ac___nowledge   2 arc___eologist   3 c___emistry

4 G___ana   5 ___onor   6 ironic___lly   7 reb___ild   8 tau___t

Brainteaser

What has two arms, two wings, two tails, three heads, three bodies, and eight legs?

Answer on page 97.

82

UNIT 7

EXTENSION

LESSON 1

Complete the sentences for yourself.

1 I've never been asked to

2 I've never been involved in

3 I've never been given

4 When I was younger, I wasn't allowed to

5 I'm not allowed to

6 When I'm older, I'll be allowed to

7 At elementary school I was taught to

8 I hope one day I'll be taught to

LESSON 2

Complete the sentences, giving your opinion using passive infinitives.

1 I think women should

2 I'm sure men ought

3 I know the environment must

4 I agree that all children deserve

5 I am beginning

6 I want

LESSON 3

Look at the role-play in exercise 7 on page 93 of the Student's Book. Write a conversation between a caller and the school.

LESSON 4

Look at exercise 9 on page 95 of the Student's Book and write two paragraphs giving the arguments for and against one of the topics which you didn't choose for your debate.

Web watch

How many female Nobel Prize winners have there been? What categories have women been most successful in? Find out by searching the Internet for *Nobel Prize Awarded Women*. Choose one female winner and research her life. Report back to your class.

Spelling

Read and complete the words from Unit 7.

The sound /ʃh/ is often written *sh* (e.g., *ship*). It can also be written *t* (e.g., *relation*). And in some words /ʃh/ is written with *c* or *ss* (e.g., *crucial, issue*).

1 crea____ion **2** extinc____ion **3** offi____ial **4** recogni____ion

5 revolu____ion **6** so____ial **7** telecommunica____ions

8 tradi____ional **9** transmi____ion

Brainteaser

From what number can you take away half and leave nothing?

Answer on page 97.

83

7 Culture

1 Reading

Read *Tips for creative writing*. Then complete with these words.

better brainstorm conversations creative criticism different draft easier empty
enjoy everywhere friends inspiration longer revise short stores unusual

Tips for creative writing

Take a notebook with you (1) _____ **you go.** As soon as you have an idea that could be used in your writing, make a note of it. You will be surprised how often you can find (2) _____ in all kinds of daily situations. Listen to other people talking in the street or in (3) _____ and coffee shops so that you get a feel for how real (4) _____ sound. Look out for (5) _____ sights or sounds that could be the start of a poem, a short story, or a video script.

Start by writing short pieces. Faced with an (6) _____ page and no ideas, many writers give up because it is easier to do something else instead. If you want to be a creative writer, you have to be determined. Stick to it and it really will get (7) _____. Try to do some writing every day, even if it's just for ten or 15 minutes, and start with (8) _____ pieces. Just a paragraph or two is enough to begin with. Soon you'll find that you can write for (9) _____. But don't overdo it! It's important to stay fresh and enthusiastic. You will write better if you (10) _____ what you are doing.

Make sure you write when you're at your most creative. When it comes to the best time to write, we are all (11) _____. Some people work better in the morning. and others have their best ideas late at night. Try writing at different times of the day in order to find out when is the best and most (12) _____ time for you.

Don't worry if you don't get it right the first time. Few writers are happy with the first story, the first paragraph, or even the first sentence that they write. Do a first (13) _____, then read it again a few days later. You can then (14) _____ or edit it to make it better. Sometimes it helps to join a writers' group where you can (15) _____ ideas and exchange your work. Feedback from other writers can be very helpful. If you don't know any other writers, use your (16) _____ and family. And don't be afraid of (17) _____. Listen to it and use it to make your work (18) _____.

84

2 Vocabulary

Read the text again and match these words and phrases with their definitions.

1 get a feel for something ☐
2 give up ☐
3 determined ☐
4 enthusiastic ☐
5 edit ☐
6 exchange ☐
7 feedback ☐
8 criticism ☐

a having a strong desire to succeed
b make changes to something written down
c negative comments about something
d learn to understand something
e information about what someone thinks about something
f excited about something
g stop doing something because it is too difficult
h to give something in return for something else

3 Comprehension

Read the tips on page 84 again and answer these questions.

1 How can you get a feel for how real conversations sound?

2 Why do many writers give up before they have started?

3 Why is it important not to write too much and become tired of it?

4 Why should you try writing at different times of the day?

5 How can joining a writers' group help you?

6 What should your attitude to criticism be?

4 Crossword

Complete the crossword puzzle and find the hidden message ↓.

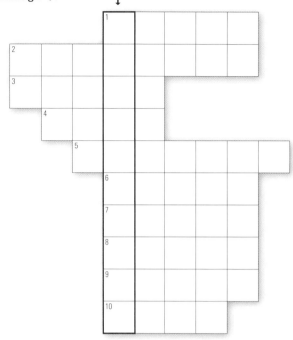

1 To be defensive is to react ... to criticism.
2 It's a good idea to carry a ... to write down ideas.
3 Unable to do anything.
4 It is important to take ... of the appearance of your work.
5 Always take time to ... on what you have written.
6 Say the words of song lyrics ... as you write them.
7 Different people find it easier to write at different ... of the day.
8 Before you start writing, you need to generate ...
9 You will need to create a storyboard to plan a ...
10 You should ... your draft to make sure there are no mistakes.

5 Writing

Write a story about a challenging experience, using these questions to help you. Try to use some of the tips on creative writing.

- Who was involved and what was the occasion?
- How did your character(s) feel at first?
- Were there any problems?
- What was the best thing about the experience?
- Did it change your character(s) in any way?

85

8 MAKING THE GRADE

1 He wasn't able to get a job

1 Reading

Read the text and complete it with these words. Then match the pictures with the paragraphs 1–4.

> ability boring burned couldn't described failed ideas
> inspiration managed missed school short were won

Famous failures—*who are they?*

❶ ....

The creator of the most famous cartoon character of all time, he revolutionized the art of animation. His movies (**1**) .... a total of 48 Academy Awards®, and he received numerous other awards and college degrees. He has been (**2**) .... as the most significant figure in graphic arts since Leonardo da Vinci. He was also the (**3**) .... behind some of the most famous theme parks in the world. However, he was fired by a newspaper editor. The editor said that he didn't have any (**4**) .... Years later, his company bought the company that owned the newspaper.

❷ ....

He was the greatest painter of the twentieth century. But his father took him out of (**5**) .... at the age of ten because all he did was paint. He (**6**) .... really read or write, and he was also terrible at math. Later, he (**7**) .... to get into art college easily, but soon left because he found it (**8**) ....

❸ ....

He created the Walkman®. But one of his first projects was a rice cooker which (**9**) .... the rice. Only 100 cookers were sold. Later, with Masaru Ibuka, he built a cheap tape recorder for schools. After its success they (**10**) .... able to start the Sony Corporation®.

❹ ....

One of the most successful basketball players in the world, he is often called "Air" because of his (**11**) .... to jump through the air to put the ball in the net. A famous sports shoe manufacturer named one of its shoes after him. But he was dropped from his high school basketball team because he was too (**12**) .... He once said, "I've (**13**) .... more than 9,000 shots in my career. I've lost almost 300 games. 26 times I've been trusted to take the game winning shot and missed. I've (**14**) .... over and over and over again in my life. And that is why I succeed."

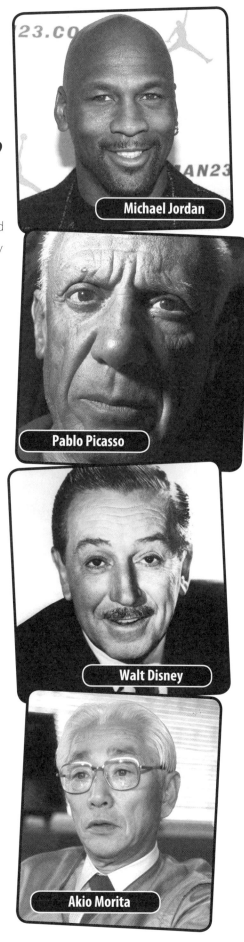

Michael Jordan

Pablo Picasso

Walt Disney

Akio Morita

UNIT 8

2 could(n't), was(n't) able to, managed to

Rewrite the sentences about "savants" using the verbs in parentheses. A "savant" is someone who has extraordinary mental abilities.

1 Daniel Tammett became a savant at the age of three, and could see numbers as shapes and colors. (be able)

2 As a child he was able to do mathematical calculations amazingly quickly. (could)

3 But his eight younger brothers and sisters could do things like kick a ball or swim better than him. (be able)

4 By the time he was 26, he had succeeded in learning six foreign languages. (manage)

5 Last year Tammett met Kim Peek, another savant, who was able to read two books at the same time. (could)

6 Recently Tammett managed to create his own language. (be able)

3 Expressing purpose

Complete with *in order to* or *so that*.

A man climbed up a ladder with his bag of tools
(1) .... repair the roof. When he reached the top, he took out his tools **(2)** .... he could start work. But he dropped one of the tools and turned **(3)** .... catch it. He held on to the ladder **(4)** .... he didn't fall. But the ladder moved. **(5)** .... save himself, he jumped off the ladder to the ground. He landed safely but the ladder began to fall. He started to run **(6)** .... get out of the way of the ladder. But it was a long, heavy ladder and it fell on top of him. As he lay on the ground, he put his hand in his pocket **(7)** .... get his cell phone **(8)** .... he could call for help. Then he realized that his phone was in the bag of tools on the roof.

4 Vocabulary

Match these words and phrases from the poem on page 101 of the Student's Book with their definitions.

> drag   earn a star   grumble   stuck in red tape   twin

1 be given a prize for being a good student

2 pull someone or something along with difficulty

3 one of two children born at the same time to one mother

4 complain, sometimes continuously

5 caught in rules which slow things down

5 Vocabulary

Compare the words in list A with the words in list B. Write *S* if they have almost the same meaning, *O* if they are opposites, and *G* if A is more general than B.

	A	B	
1	music	concerto	*G*
2	person	youth	
3	failure	success	
4	totally	completely	
5	fail	pass	

6 Vocabulary

Match the words in list A with the words in list B.

	A	B		
1	approved	composer	**1**	*approved school*
2	classical	poet	**2**	
3	entrance	school	**3**	
4	problem	examination	**4**	
5	rap	student	**5**	

7 Pronunciation

Do they rhyme (✓) or not (✗)?

1	fairly	nearly	✗
2	deaf	thief	☐
3	earn	turn	☐
4	planned	band	☐
5	youth	truth	☐

> **Extension** Write a paragraph about a famous person but don't use their name. Show it to another student to guess who it is.

87

8 MAKING THE GRADE

2 They had to pay

1 Reading

Read *School 50 years ago and in the future* and complete the text with these words.

> able   behavior   compulsory   didn't   had   have
> respected   strict   to   uniform   weren't   won't

SCHOOL 50 YEARS AGO AND IN THE FUTURE

Three students remember:

"We had to wear our bright blue and yellow school (1) _____, even when we went to school on Saturday morning. And we had to raise our caps when we met a teacher. Saturday morning exercises were (2) _____. I hated exercises, but I did what I was told. I (3) _____ my teachers, and more than half a century later, am grateful to them for my interest in music and literature."

"The teaching was very (4) _____. The teachers stood at the front of the class with all our desks facing them. When we did something wrong, the teacher hit us on the hand with a ruler. They (5) _____ need to do that very often because we were so scared of them. The school meals were terrible, and we (6) _____ to eat everything up—you (7) _____ able to leave anything on your plate."

"I remember feeling very shy when I went to school for the first time. We had 46 children in my class, and one teacher. There weren't any (8) _____ problems, although one boy had (9) _____ stand outside the principal's office for making noise in class. I'm a teacher now myself, and things are certainly very different!"

Experts predict:

And if students get their way in the school of the future, this is what will happen. Teachers will (10) _____ to go to school, even if they're sick—they (11) _____ be able to stay at home. This will mean that students won't have new teachers who don't know their names. Finally, students will be (12) _____ to choose one subject and study it all day and won't have to keep changing subjects.

2 Modal expressions in the past

Complete with *had to, was(n't) able to, were(n't) able to,* or *didn't need to.*

1 A year ago they _____ speak French at all, but now they can.
2 When I started school, I _____ learn to tie my shoes myself.
3 She knew she _____ worry but she couldn't help it.
4 He spoke so quickly that I _____ follow what he said.
5 I didn't know that you _____ ride a horse. When did you learn?
6 She said that they _____ help, but it would be nice if they did.
7 The train was late so he _____ get to the meeting on time.

UNIT 8

3 Modal expressions in the future

Complete the sentences with *won't have to,*
will/won't be able to, or *will need to.*

1 She travels free on the buses now but she
.... when she's 16.

2 He doesn't iron his own clothes now but he
.... learn how to
when he leaves home.

3 I can't pick up e-mails on my cell phone but I
.... when I get a
new smartphone.

4 You .... wait much
longer—the show is about to start.

5 When .... you ....
let me know the answer?

6 You .... think
carefully—it's a big decision.

7 Unless you listen, you ....
remember the instructions.

8 She .... leave early
in order to catch the last train.

4 *didn't need to* and *needn't have*

Complete with *didn't need to* or *needn't have* and the
correct form of the verbs.

1 You .... (call) her because
she already knew about it.

2 It was Saturday morning, and she knew that she
.... (get up) early.

3 We .... (show) our ID cards
to get into the club.

4 They .... (order) a taxi—it
was a waste of money.

5 I .... (bother) to put on my
new dress—no one noticed!

6 She .... (bring) him
flowers—everyone had already sent him some.

> You needn't have brought me flowers.

5 Vocabulary

Find 12 words to do with education in the word square.

C	U	R	R	I	C	U	L	U	M
L	N	E	D	E	G	R	E	E	H
A	I	L	E	S	S	O	N	R	S
S	F	G	S	O	U	A	R	U	T
S	O	R	K	F	B	Q	U	L	U
F	R	A	G	R	J	H	A	E	D
G	M	D	C	T	E	A	C	H	Y
E	F	E	Y	S	C	H	O	O	L
S	S	C	H	E	D	U	L	E	E

6 Vocabulary

Match the words in list A with the words in list B and
write seven compound words.

A		B		
1	book	work	1	*bookstore*
2	class	board	2	
3	tuition	line	3	
4	on	sheet	4	
5	solar	store	5	
6	spread	costs	6	
7	white	system	7	

7 Vocabulary

Match the verbs in list A with the words in list B. Then
write the phrases.

A		B		
1	get	your turn	1	*get married*
2	pay	tuition costs	2	
3	wait	action	3	
4	clean	married	4	
5	study	your room	5	
6	take	a subject	6	

8 Pronunciation

Write the number of syllables and mark the stress.

■
classwork *2*   comfort ......   curriculum ......

interactive ......   pressure ......   spreadsheet ......

submarine ......   waterproof ......   whiteboard ......

> **Extension** Write sentences using all the
> compound words in exercise 6.

89

8

3 It made me feel great

MAKING THE GRADE

1 Reading

Read the text and complete it with these words.

admire amazing dream inspired let made
musical online progressed succeed star tool

Brad — (1) _____ of the future!

Brad, tell us a little about yourself.
I'm 19 years old and I make electro pop music. I've finished three albums (though I still haven't signed with a record company). I'm not in a band—I play on my own.

And how did you get started?
I began writing and playing music when I was six. My parents never (2) _____ me—I just did it on my own. I've become more familiar with computers and it's great to use them as a (3) _____ for making music. Computers offer so many opportunities to be creative—they really (4) _____ me be myself.

Who were your (5) _____ influences?
There are so many—Little Boots, Depeche Mode, Owl City—all these bands and artists have really (6) _____ me to work harder at my music. I really (7) _____ them and want to be like them. I used to feel that my music would never be as good as theirs. But now I know that with the right attitude I can (8) _____!

What successes have you had, and what about the future?
I'm very proud of the fact that thousands of people have listened to my music (9) _____ on my website. My music has (10) _____ over the years, and I want to go as far as possible with it. A favorite (11) _____ of mine is to go into a club and hear my music and see everyone enjoying it.

And your favorite things in life?
Music—it's my life—my family and all my friends. I also love acting—it's an (12) _____ feeling being on stage.

2 *make, let,* and *be allowed to*

Complete with the correct form of *make, let,* or *be allowed to*.

1   The smell of fresh bread always _____ me feel hungry.

2   My new cell phone _____ me make calls anywhere in the world.

3   I (not) _____ tell you the answer.

4   Being on stage _____ Brad feel great.

5   Yesterday she _____ to apologize for being rude.

6   _____ you _____ use this entrance or is it only for actors?

7   They promised to _____ me have an answer soon.

8   My parents (not) _____ me borrow their car.

90

UNIT **8**

3 *make, let,* and *be allowed to*

Rewrite the sentences with the correct form of the verbs.

1 We can't use cell phones in class. (allow)

2 They had to train hard before the game. (make)

3 I allowed my brother to borrow my calculator. (let)

4 Did they force him to return the money? (make)

5 At my last school we were forbidden to wear jeans. (allow)

6 My parents used to allow me to stay up late on Saturday nights. (let)

7 Global warming is causing the ocean to rise. (make)

8 Why won't you allow me to have a second chance? (let)

4 Vocabulary

Complete the sentences with the correct form of these verbs.

| come save stay take turn write |

1 Kezza's first song .... into her head while she was out walking.

2 Kezza says when you're writing a song, you just have to let it .... shape.

3 If you don't have enough money to buy a guitar, you have to .... up.

4 If an idea for a song comes to you in a dream, ... it down.

5 If you play your music too loud, your parents will tell you to .... it down.

6 How late at night do your parents let you .... up?

5 Vocabulary

Match these words and phrases with their definitions.

| chord finger picking hum lyrics around the clock |

1 words of a song ....

2 produce a tune without opening your lips or making words ....

3 all day and night ....

4 two or more musical notes played together ....

5 playing the strings of a guitar with the fingers ....

6 Vocabulary

Compare the words in list A with the words in list B. Write *S* if they have almost the same meaning, *O* if they are opposites, and *G* if A is more general than B.

	A	B	
1	practice	rehearse	*S*
2	words	lyrics	
3	strong	weak	
4	styles	kinds	
5	perform	sing	
6	generally	usually	

7 Vocabulary

Match the verbs with these words and phrases.

| a chord hard at shape true to yourself words to a tune |

1 be ....

2 fit ....

3 play ....

4 take ....

5 work ....

8 Pronunciation

Write the number of syllables and mark the stress.

advice *2*   concerned ....   hummed ....

influence ....   instrument ....   lyrics ....

perform ....   personal ....   songwriting ....

> **Extension** Who or what are the strongest influences in your life? Write a paragraph about them.

91

8 MAKING THE GRADE

4 Integrated Skills
Making an application

1 Reading

Read the website information about International Volunteers and complete the text with these words.

accommodation   advance   airfare   allowance   application   contribution   education   experience
fundraise   host   opportunity   projects   skills   successful   vaccinations   volunteer

www.internationalvolunteers.org

| article | discussion | **edit this page** | history |

- Main page
- Community Portal
- Featured articles
- Current events
- Recent changes
- Random article
- Help

search

[Go] [Search]

toolbox
- What links here
- Related changes
- Upload file
- Special pages
- Printable version
- Permanent link
- Cite this article

in other languages
- Deutsch
- Eesti
- Español
- Français
- Galego
- 한국어
- Bahasa Indonesia
- Italiano
- עברית
- Nederlands
- 日本語
- Polski
- Português

INTERNATIONAL VOLUNTEERS

International Volunteers is a unique international organization which brings together volunteers from all over the world to work in developing countries. We organize (**1**) .... worldwide with a particular emphasis on health, (**2**) ...., and community support—recent locations have included India, Kenya, Guatemala, and Uzbekistan. Volunteers work in teams and have the (**3**) .... to learn new skills and meet new friends, while making an important (**4**) .... to local communities.

YOU
✓ must be between 17 and 24
✓ can (**5**) .... for four weeks to six months
✓ have to (**6**) .... $1,000 towards the cost
✓ stay with a local (**7**) .... family during your time as a volunteer
✓ need to be able to speak English

WE
✓ pay for your food, (**8**) ...., and return (**9**) ....
✓ provide a weekly (**10**) ....
✓ organize (**11**) .... and medical protection where appropriate
✓ train you in the (**12**) .... you need to help the local community
✓ give you constant support during your volunteer period

"The best (**13**) .... of my life!" Silvana, Italy   "I'm really glad I did it." Don, USA
"Don't miss this fantastic opportunity!" Ewa, Poland

Click here to find out more.

How to apply
- Fill out an (**14**) .... form.
  Click here to download.
- Write a letter, saying what kind of volunteer work you want and where you'd like to work. Write about your skills, abilities, and interests and say why you think you would be a (**15**) .... volunteer.

- Mail your letter and completed form to:
  INTERNATIONAL VOLUNTEERS
  9611 14th Street
  Washington, D.C. 20009
- You should apply at least six months in (**16**) .... of the time you want to volunteer.

UNIT 8

2 Writing

Leo Stearns decides to apply to *International Volunteers*. Read the notes about him below, and then write his letter of application.

Age 17. Address 21 Hilltop Road, Skokie, IL 60077. Wants to work for four weeks in July/August during summer vacation. Would like to work on an educational project in Latin America. Speaks good Spanish, plays the guitar, enjoys soccer and swimming. Likes working on a team, gets along well with people.

3 Crossword

Complete the crossword puzzle.

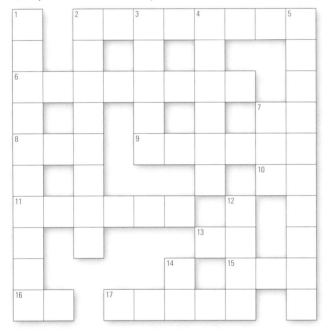

Across →

2 Marco Polo traveled to Asia in the 13th century and … China. (10)
6 Children go to school to be … (8)
7 Will you … able to come to my party? (2)
8 We … up some posters on the classroom wall. (3)
9 I'd love to … around the world. (6)
10 Don't worry about the exam—I'm sure you'll … well. (2)
11 Can you … what you wear at school? (6)
13 We saved money … that we could go on vacation. (2)
15 The car stopped because it … out of gas. (3)
16 Will you be able to … your homework tonight? (2)
17 A nightmare is a bad … (5)

Down ↓

1 It was totally …—a complete surprise! (10)
2 E=mc² is a very famous … (8)
3 Volunteers often … trees in parks. (5)
4 *Tosca* is one of Puccini's best-known … (6)
5 Many volunteers work overseas in … countries. (10)
7 It's nice to sleep in a comfortable … (3)
12 Please use a black pen to fill in the application … (4)
14 Hello, could you put … through to the manager, please? (2)

LEARNER INDEPENDENCE

Word creation

When you are trying to express yourself in English, you can use intelligent guesswork to create new words with prefixes and suffixes, and by forming compound nouns. For example:

- Add the same prefix to each of these verbs so that they mean "do it again."

  consider   open   print   sell   visit   wind

- Form "people" nouns ending in the same suffix from each of these words.

  cycle   guitar   real   reception   sociology   special

- You may not know what these items are called in English. Try to guess the compound nouns.

Now use a dictionary to check your answers.

Extensive reading

Read an English book and imagine you are one of the characters. Write your diary for the last day of the story, and say how you feel.

93

8 MAKING THE GRADE

Inspired EXTRA!

CONSOLIDATION

LESSON 1

Complete with *could(n't)*, *was(n't) able*, or *managed to*.

I have always been afraid of water and never learned to swim or scuba dive. But one day I (**1**) .... forget about being scared and went to the local swimming pool. Soon, to my surprise, I (**2**) .... to scuba dive. I (**3**) .... believe it! So I started to try other things which I thought I (**4**) .... to do, like skydiving and paragliding. It was so easy, as long as I (**5**) .... think about something other than being frightened. I didn't tell anyone that I (**6**) .... skydive and paraglide. It was my secret. My friends thought that I (**7**) .... to do anything daring, but I knew that I (**8**) ....!

LESSON 2

Complete with *had to*, *was able to*, *won't be able to*, *didn't need to*, or *will need to*.

1 Because I lived next to the school I .... go by bus.

2 When you move away, we .... see each other so often.

3 I didn't realize that I .... finish the essay by today, and now it's too late.

4 If you want to be on the team, you .... train harder.

5 I .... solve the problem easily.

6 Everyone was angry because they .... wait until the last student had finished.

7 I don't know the answer. I .... think about it some more and let you know.

8 You .... say thank you. I enjoyed helping.

LESSON 3

Complete with the correct form of *make, let*, or *be allowed to*.

1 Does your school .... you wear what you like?

2 Listening to the music last night .... me want to dance.

3 .... I .... ask a question now?

4 They .... to pick up all the trash by the police officer.

5 From now on you .... (not) check in more than 20 kg of luggage on this airline.

6 I'm not sure. Can I .... you know tomorrow?

LESSON 4

Match these words with their definitions.

1 aftershave   **a** lasting for a short period of time

2 applicant   **b** liquid with nice smell which women put on their skin

3 certificate

4 perfume   **c** someone who applies for something

5 short-term   **d** not having any weight

6 single   **e** create a picture of something in your mind

7 visualize

8 weightlessness   **f** liquid with nice smell which men put on their faces

   g not married

   h official paper saying that something is true

Spelling

Correct the spelling of these words from Unit 8 by doubling one letter in each word.

1 aplication   **2** chil-out   **3** confesion   **4** curiculum

5 embarassed   **6** hopeles   **7** mentaly   **8** maried

9 oportunity   **10** presure   **11** prize-winer

12 spreadshet   **13** ref   **14** totaly   **15** volunter

Brainteaser

A man rode into town on Friday. He stayed for three nights and then left on Friday. How come?

Answer on page 97.

94

UNIT 8

EXTENSION

LESSON 1

Complete these sentences for yourself.

1 I wasn't able to .... until I was ....

2 One thing I've never managed to do is ....

3 How much do I know about computers? Well, I'm able to ....

4 Until I went to high school I couldn't ....

5 When I was .... , I could ....

6 Learning to .... was difficult for me, but I finally managed to ....

LESSON 2

Complete these sentences for yourself.

1 Something I was able to do in the past but can't do now is ....

2 Something which I did in the past although I didn't have to do it was ....

3 Something which worried me but which I needn't have worried about was ....

4 Something which I don't need to do now but will need to do in the future is ....

5 Something which I don't have to do now and hope I won't have to do in the future is ....

LESSON 3

Read *Kezza—a girl in a million!* on page 104 of the Student's Book. Write questions for these answers about Kezza.

1 Who ....
Beyoncé, Alicia Keys, and Adele.

2 What ....
Inspired.

3 What ....
She was out walking.

4 When ....
When she was 14.

5 How ....
She saved up to buy it.

6 Which ....
Sometimes the lyrics, sometimes the music.

LESSON 4

Look at exercise 5 on page 107 of the Student's Book and write the telephone interview between an applicant and a worker at ReefAid.

Web watch

Benjamin Zephaniah often uses Jamaican English in his writing. In his poem *Talking Turkeys*, he argues for turkey rights at Christmas time. Search for *Benjamin Zephaniah* on the Internet. Try to figure out what some of the words in *Talking Turkeys* mean.

Spelling

Read and complete the words from Unit 8.

The sound /əl/ at the end of a word can be written -*al*, -*ul*, -*el*, and -*le*.

1 classic........ 2 comfortab........ 3 cor........ 4 crumb........
5 glob........ 6 loc........ 7 ment........ 8 music........
9 nov........ 10 person........ 11 sing........ 12 successf........
13 thoughtf........ 14 tot........

Brainteaser

What's odd about this paragraph? Look at it hard—don't just whizz through it quickly. You'll find that it's most unusual, although nothing in it is wrong. If you study its vocabulary, you should spot what's so unusual about it. Can you say what it is? Actually, it isn't so difficult—this isn't a hoax!

Answer on page 97.

REVIEW
UNITS 7-8

1 Read the magazine article. Then read the sentences and choose *True*, *False*, or *Doesn't say*.

I swapped a paperclip for a house
—Kyle MacDonald

I started with one red paperclip on July 12, 2005. I was in Montreal, half-heartedly looking for jobs, when I saw the paperclip on my desk. I wondered what would happen if, instead of applying for a job, I tried to exchange it.

I posted a picture of that paperclip on my website, oneredpaperclip.com, and then traded with two local ladies for a pen shaped like a fish. I exchanged the pen for a doorknob, and the doorknob for a camping stove. I always made the trades in person—it was less about the trade itself than about meeting up. The Canadian media picked up my story, and suddenly the website was being visited by 100,000 people a day. That's when I made the claim that I was going to go on trading until I got a house.

Eventually, I had a snow globe from the punk band Kiss, which I traded with the producer of a Hollywood movie for a small speaking role. The producer collects snow globes and realized that publicity could be generated by the trade.

Then the community development officer of a little town called Kipling in central Canada heard about the story. Kipling's population had been falling and a number of houses had been empty for over a year. He saw making a trade as a way to attract media and tourism. The town offered me a house on Main Street in exchange for the movie role. I said, "Deal."

The first time my girlfriend and I came to the town, it was overwhelming: 500 people were standing in front of the house to welcome us. It was exactly one year from when I had made that first trade.

It's hard to have a private life when you've got an address that people around the world know about. It is a private home, but it's a semi-public tourist attraction at the same time. We're visited by more than 20 people a day. I'm not good in front of a crowd, but when people have driven two hours to see the house, you want to give them some time.

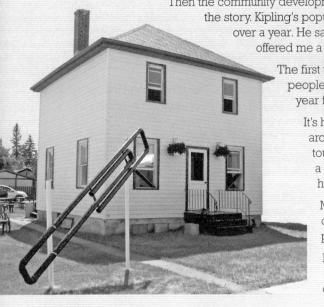

My girlfriend and a bunch of friends are living here, too. I've never owned a house before, so we're enjoying being able to take out walls, painting, and repairing it.

Last weekend, Kipling held open auditions for the movie role. A local 19-year-old guy got the part, and thousands of visitors from across the country came to Kipling for the party. The town has really benefited.

1 Kyle MacDonald was short of money when he decided to exchange the paperclip.
  A True   **B** False   **C** Doesn't say

2 He exchanged the paperclip for a fish.
  A True   **B** False   **C** Doesn't say

3 He met all the people he traded with.
  A True   **B** False   **C** Doesn't say

4 Once the media got hold of the story, Kyle's website was visited by a million people a day.
  A True   **B** False   **C** Doesn't say

5 Kyle was offered work in a movie.
  A True   **B** False   **C** Doesn't say

6 Kyle managed to get a house after more than a dozen trades.
  A True   **B** False   **C** Doesn't say

7 He was amazed by the welcome when he first arrived in Kipling.
  A True   **B** False   **C** Doesn't say

8 He feels he has to talk to people who visit the house on Main Street.
  A True   **B** False   **C** Doesn't say

9 He lived in an apartment before moving to Kipling.
  A True   **B** False   **C** Doesn't say

10 Trading with Kyle has done Kipling a lot of good.
  A True   **B** False   **C** Doesn't say

2 Complete with the correct form of the words in capitals.

1 The weather in the U.S. is becoming _____ warm. INCREASE

2 She received an award in _____ of her achievements. RECOGNIZE

3 J.K. Rowling is an _____ successful author. USUAL

4 The giant panda is one of several _____ species. DANGER

5 The person who is the best _____ will get the job. APPLY

6 The criminal made a full _____ to the police. CONFESS

3 Complete the second sentence so that it means the same as the first sentence.

1 An ambulance took the injured boy to the hospital.
The injured boy _____

2 My new bicycle has been stolen!
Someone _____

3 We couldn't understand what the man said.
We weren't _____

4 He succeeded in getting into college.
He managed _____

5 It wasn't necessary for you to buy so much food.
You needn't _____

6 The driver was made to stop the car by the police.
The police _____

4 Find the word that is different.

1 ladder platform steps stairs
2 biology chemistry physics scientist
3 alarm disaster earthquake flood
4 comet planet rocket subject
5 century decade period year
6 accommodation guesthouse hostel hotel
7 ferry jet submarine yacht
8 idiom phrase linguist slang

Answers to Brainteasers

UNIT 7
Consolidation A man on a horse holding a chicken.
Extension 8

UNIT 8
Consolidation The man's horse was called Friday.
Extension The paragraph contains every letter of the alphabet except *E*, which is the commonest letter in the English language.

LEARNER INDEPENDENCE
SELF ASSESSMENT

Vocabulary

1 Draw this chart in your notebook. How many words can you write in each category?

More than 10? Good! *More than 12?* Very good!
More than 15? Excellent!

Education	
Cell phones	
Science	

2 Put the words in order to make expressions from the phrasebooks in Lesson 4 in Units 7 and 8.

1 put through I'll you
I'll put you through.

2 up keep it
_____

3 done can be anything
_____

4 take I message can a
_____

5 I'm as concerned as far ...
_____

6 mad drove me it
_____

7 you to up it's
_____

Check your answers.
8/8 Excellent! *6/8* Very good! *4/8* Try again!

My learning diary
In Units 7 and 8:
My favorite topic is _____

My favorite picture is _____

The three lessons I like most are _____

My favorite activity or exercise is _____

Something I don't understand is _____

Something I want to learn more about is _____

1 Bear Creek

Monday 7:00 a.m.

Look at the picture. Where are the boys? What are they doing?

I'm asleep in bed and I'm dreaming. I'm dreaming that I'm on a plane with my best friend Tony. We're traveling to a movie festival in New York. The best thing is that our movie is in the festival. Through the window we can see Manhattan. We arrive, and a long black car is waiting for us at the airport. We get in.

"Wake up, Mike," said Tony. It wasn't a dream. We really were on a plane flying over New York.

Through the window I could see the tall buildings of Manhattan and, yes, it really did look just like it looks in the movies.

This wasn't our first visit to a big city—we come from one. Tony and I live in Toronto in Canada. Toronto looks a little like New York, especially downtown. In fact, it's always full of movie companies that are shooting movies there. And when you see the movie, they pretend it's New York. But you know it isn't, because you can recognize that it's Queen Street, Toronto.

But this was the real New York. Tony and I were there for the Student Movie Festival and we were in the contest for Best Student Documentary. Our movie was called *Living in Bear Creek*. Bear Creek is in the north of Canada and it's really wild there. You can walk for days and not see anyone. And the reason why you don't see many people is because of the bears. That's why it's called Bear Creek. And the bears are dangerous. It's a part of the world where people struggle every day to survive.

Tony and I spent six months there. The only other people were the men who cut down the trees—the loggers. We lived with them and filmed their lives. Their lives are difficult and it's cold, extremely cold. After working all day, the men have little to do in the evenings, since there aren't any coffee shops or movie theaters. There's nothing—just trees and a few dangerous bears.

We spent a long time filming in Bear Creek because we wanted to show what life was really like there. We didn't want to fly in and interview a few men and then fly out again. We wanted to show the whole picture. And now our movie was in the Student Movie Festival.

We arrived at JFK International Airport and there was a car to take us into the city. It was a long black car. So sometimes your dreams can come true. We felt like movie directors.

We arrived at our hotel and, suddenly, everything wasn't so great. On the contrary, it was terrible. A woman named Teresa from the Movie Festival welcomed us to New York. Teresa had some bad news for us. "Unfortunately, your movie is missing," she said.

"What do you mean—'missing'?" I asked. "Where is it?"

"We don't know. It was locked in my room with the other movies yesterday. Today I checked the movies and it wasn't there," Teresa said. "I guess someone took it. But why? And how did they get into my room?"

I didn't know the answers to her questions. I looked around. The hotel was busy, but I saw someone I recognized. A man in black. "He was on our plane, too," I thought.

"What are we going to do?" Teresa asked.

"It's OK," Tony replied. "The missing movie doesn't matter. I've got a copy on my laptop at home."

Tony smiled, took out his phone and turned it on. The phone rang immediately. It was his mother, and she was in tears.

Tony stopped smiling. "What is it?" he asked.

"Someone broke into the house last night when your father and I were out," she said.

"What did they steal?" asked Tony.

"That's what's so strange," his mother answered. "They didn't take anything of ours at all. But your room ... all your books and papers are on the floor. And they've taken your laptop."

Why did someone take Mike and Tony's movie? And who is the man in black?

98

2 Bear Creek

Monday 9:30 a.m.

Look at the picture. What is the woman telling Mike and Tony? Who is the man on the right of the picture?

Tony's mother was still crying. She sounded really upset.

"What is it?" Tony asked again. "What else has happened?"

"It's Kelly," said his mother.

Kelly is Tony's sister. She's 17, two years younger than Tony and me and she's great. I've known Tony's family all my life, and Kelly is like my little sister, too.

"I told you that your father and I went out last night," Tony's mother said. "Well, when we got back she had disappeared. We've been waiting all night for her to call, but we haven't heard from her."

"She's probably staying with friends," Tony told his mother.

"I've been calling her friends all morning," his mother told him. "But no one's seen her since yesterday. She's not answering her cell phone. I've been so worried. The police are looking for her, too. And then your movie …" She started crying again.

Tony tried to say the right thing, but it wasn't easy. I felt bad, too. Here we were in New York, Kelly was missing, and we didn't have a movie. We couldn't have felt worse. We'd filmed in Bear Creek for six months, and had been working on the movie ever since. Now the movie was finished and someone had taken it.

"Why?" I asked Tony after he had finished his call. "Why did someone take our movie?"

"Why did someone steal my laptop?" he replied, but there were no answers to our questions. Then I remembered something. Something wonderful.

"Wait, I'll call Mom," I said. "I've just remembered. I've also got a copy of the movie on my computer!"

I turned on my phone and there were lots of messages from my mother. I called her.

"Thank goodness," Mom said. "I've been waiting for you to turn your phone on for hours."

"Have you heard about Tony's house and Kelly?" I asked her.

"Yes, it's terrible," she agreed. "But there's something else."

What? What else had happened?

"Last night a detective came here," said Mom. "He told us about the robbery at Tony's house and asked about your movie. So I showed him the copy on your computer. He was very happy and took the computer away with him. Then, an hour later, another police officer came here and I told him about the first detective. Then I realized what I'd done. I hadn't asked the first detective for his ID. He wasn't a real police officer—no one knows who he was. He'd just been pretending to be a police officer. And he's taken your computer with your movie on it!"

I said goodbye and told Tony what my mother had said. Neither of us knew what to do. Our world had exploded. This morning we had had a great future, but now we had nothing.

"Excuse me, Mike and Tony." It was Teresa. She had been standing beside us while we'd been on the phone. But we'd forgotten all about her. We apologized and told Teresa what had happened in Toronto. She was very sympathetic.

"That's terrible," she said. "But you have to find out what's been going on, and why someone wants your movie. What did you see at Bear Creek?"

"Trees," I answered. "Just trees."

"Think," said Teresa, "and call me if you need me." She gave us her number and said goodbye.

But while Tony and I were talking, I saw the man in black again.

"Do you see that man?" I asked Tony. "He's been watching us ever since we came in. He's been listening to our phone calls."

"Let's get out of here," Tony replied.

We walked out onto a New York street. We didn't know where we were going, but we just wanted to move. As we walked down the street, I looked back and there was the man in black. He was following us.

What was in Mike and Tony's movie? Why do you think the man in black is following them? And where is Kelly?

3 Bear Creek

Monday 10:00 a.m.

Look at the picture. What are Mike and Tony doing? What is the man in the background doing?

The man in black was following us. We walked extremely fast down one street and then another, but he was still behind us.

"What are we going to do?" asked Tony. "He'll catch us sooner or later."

Then I saw a small park on the left, where some teenagers were skateboarding.

"Quick!" I said and pulled Tony into the park. I ran up to a couple of the skateboarders and asked, "Can we borrow your caps, jackets, and skateboards for five minutes?"

"Sure," they said. "Who's following you?" These were New York teenagers—they weren't stupid.

"Just some guy," I told them.

"No problem," they said. "Ten dollars—each." We gave them the money and they lent us their jackets and caps. We put them on and started skateboarding.

"What a good idea!" Tony laughed. "The man in black won't recognize us now."

Just then, the man in black came into the park and looked around. Suddenly, I wasn't sure that skateboarding was such a good idea after all. Tony and I pulled our caps down so that he couldn't see our faces.

Then the man in black took out his phone and spoke to someone. A few minutes later, a fast, new, white car stopped outside the park. The man in black walked very slowly over to it. He looked around once more and then got in.

"He's from the police," said one of the teenagers. "Are you running from them?"

"No," Tony said. "We don't know who he is, but he's not a police officer."

"He looked like a police officer," said the teenager. We laughed, gave him and his friend their caps, jackets, and skateboards back, and left the park.

"Where are we going to go now?" asked Tony. "Should we go back to the hotel?"

Just then, Tony's phone rang. It was Kelly.

"Kelly! Where are you? Mom's going crazy with worry!" Tony shouted.

"I'm in New York," said Kelly.

"New York? Are you OK?" Tony asked her.

"I'm tired and dirty, but more importantly, I have a DVD with me. And your movie's on it," she told him.

"What great news!" said Tony. "It's such a surprise. We thought we'd lost all the copies. But how did you …?"

"I can't answer any questions now," said Kelly. "Is anyone following you?"

"There was a man but we lost him."

"Good," said Kelly. "Something really bad is going on. Where should we meet? Someone's probably watching your hotel."

"What about the top of the Empire State Building?" I said—it was the one place I knew in New York.

"OK," Kelly agreed. "I'll go there immediately. It's not far from where I am now."

Tony called his mother to tell her that Kelly was alive and well, and in New York. Somehow I wasn't surprised about Kelly.

She'd always been crazy—great, but crazy, too. She played the guitar extremely well, and was also a genius on computers—she could do anything on them.

Tony checked our New York guidebook. "Buses go from here to the Empire State Building every 15 minutes," he said and looked at his watch. "So the next one leaves in five minutes."

As we waited for the bus I got the feeling that someone was watching us. I looked around, but I couldn't see anyone.

"I'll feel safer when we get on the bus," I said to Tony. "Then we'll know that no one is following us."

The bus came and we got on. No one else got on behind us.

"Everything's going to be all right," I said to Tony with a smile. In fact, I sounded more confident than I really was. I felt scared and I didn't like the feeling. Then I saw the white car behind the bus.

Why is someone following them? And what's Kelly doing in New York?

4 Bear Creek

Monday 11:30 a.m.

Look at the picture. Who is the girl? Why is she running?

It took 15 minutes for the bus to get to the Empire State Building. When we arrived, we joined a long line to get in.

"We'll never find Kelly among all these people," I said. "And if we stay in the line, it'll be ages before we go up."

Tony called Kelly. "Where are you?" he asked her.

"I'm near the front of the line," she said. "They say that our group is going up in about 30 minutes."

"If you go up then, you'll be down here again before we get to the front of the line," Tony told her. "That's crazy. Let's meet outside the door of the 33rd Street entrance in two minutes instead."

We left the line and, as we did, so did a tall man. He was 20 meters behind us when we found Kelly. She looked like someone who had traveled all night and needed a shower. Kelly started to explain why she was in New York.

"I wish we had time to talk now, but we don't. That tall man's following us!" I told her. We ran across Herald Square and into a big department store named Macy's. It was full of people. We ran quickly through the store and out of a door on the other side. The tall man didn't see us leave the store. We turned and walked fast down 7th Avenue.

There was an Internet café on the next corner. We could sit there and watch the street without being seen. Kelly ordered coffee and cake, and we relaxed for the first time since we'd arrived in New York.

"So tell us what happened," said Tony.

"If you let me have something to eat, I'll tell you everything," said Kelly. "I'm starving! I've been traveling since late last night and haven't eaten a thing."

She ate two pieces of cake, and then she began her story.

"It was about nine o'clock last night," said Kelly. "Mom and Dad were out. They'd gone to see a movie, and I was in my tree house."

Kelly's father had made her a tree house. It's like a real room, but it's halfway up a tree. Kelly can play the guitar there for hours without driving the family crazy. And with wireless technology she can communicate with people in the house, and follow what's going on.

"I'd had a great idea," Kelly went on. "I'd copied your movie on to my laptop and taken it up to the tree house. It's a great movie, but I thought it would be better if it had music. So I was recording some guitar music to go with the movie."

"The movie's fine as it is," Tony pointed out. "It doesn't need music."

"Listen," said Kelly. "If you keep interrupting, you'll miss out on the rest of the story. Now you know that up in the tree I can hear what's happening in the house below. Well, I was working on the music for your movie when I heard voices from the house. 'This is his room,' a man was saying. 'Now where's the movie?' 'I think it's on this laptop,' another voice said. 'Yes, here's the movie.' 'OK,' said the first man, 'now we must carry out Mr. Cross's orders. He doesn't want anyone to see that movie. You know what his orders are. Destroy the movie and then destroy the boys. So wipe out the movie on the laptop.' 'But if I wipe out the movie, people will know why we've been here. On the other hand, if we steal the laptop, they'll think it was an ordinary robbery,' the other voice replied. 'OK, you're right,' the first man said. 'Let's make it look like a robbery and take the laptop with us. These boys are going to be very sorry …' He sounded really horrible," Kelly added.

Tony and I looked at each other. We were both really frightened.

"Who is Mr. Cross and why is he doing this?" asked Tony.

"If I knew, I'd tell you. The men didn't say, and I certainly didn't go into the house to ask them," replied his sister. "It's something that's on your movie."

"But we didn't film anything except trees and loggers," said Tony. "And the loggers loved our movie. I just don't understand."

"So what did you do?" I asked Kelly.

"I just waited until I heard them leave, and then a bit longer, in case they came back. Then, as soon as I was sure, I copied your movie onto a DVD and left. I got a flight to New York. And here I am."

Why does Mr. Cross want to destroy the boys? What's on the movie that he doesn't like?

101

5 Bear Creek

Monday 12:30 p.m.

Look at the picture. What is Kelly telling Mike? What is Tony doing?

"You must have filmed something while you were in Bear Creek," Kelly said for the second time. "You're just not thinking."

"We'd be aware of it if we'd filmed something important," I said.

"We don't have to look at the movie again, we know it so well," Tony agreed, "and I tell you nothing happened in Bear Creek! We didn't see anything."

"You must have seen something," Kelly said again. "You just don't remember what it was."

"I wish I knew, but I can't think of anything," I told her.

"Then why does this Mr. Cross want to destroy the movie and the two of you?" she asked us.

"If we knew the answer to that question, we'd know what to do," Tony replied.

But the truth was, we didn't know. "And what did Mr. Cross mean by 'destroy'?" I asked myself. Was he going to kill us? It was very frightening.

"Let's pay for these coffees and go," I said.

"There's an ATM over there," said Tony. "I'll get some money out."

He came back to our table a minute later. "This is getting stranger and stranger. If you'd told me yesterday that this could happen, I wouldn't have believed you," he told us.

"Yesterday I had $250 in the bank. Today it seems I have $100,000!"

"It must be a mistake," I said.

"It isn't," said Tony. "You go and check your account."

"OK," I said. "I know what I have in the bank—nothing. I bought a new pair of jeans to wear here in New York and gave my last $20 to the skateboarders in the park." I went to the ATM and put in my card. I had $100,000, too!

"Great," said Kelly. "We can all go shopping. I saw an amazing jacket in Macy's as we ran through."

"If only it was that simple," said Tony. "It's not our money. If we spent the money, we'd never get away with it. Something really strange is going on."

Then his phone rang. It was his mother.

I couldn't hear what she said, but Tony kept saying: "What?" Then he said, "Yes, don't worry, she's safe here." Kelly said "Yes. Tell Mom I'm fine," and then Tony said "What?" again really loudly. Finally he said, "You can't believe that! It's just not true!" Then he turned off his phone.

"What?" Kelly and I both asked. "What was that about? What did she say?"

"The police are there, at home," Tony told Kelly. "They think Mike and I are involved in crime. They want the police here in New York to arrest us."

"But we haven't done anything wrong," I complained.

"I know that," said Tony angrily. "But they think we have. Someone must have told the police about the money in our bank accounts, and they want to know how we got it."

"We'd like to know that ourselves," I said. "This is all crazy."

There was a TV on the wall of the café, and as we were talking we suddenly saw our faces on the screen. A man was saying, "These boys are wanted by the police here in New York and back home in Toronto. If you see them, call this number."

"It's Mr. Cross," I said to Tony. "*He's* done this. He's behind this elaborate trick."

"But how do we prove it?" he asked. "We don't even know who Mr. Cross is."

"The answer has to be in the movie," Kelly said again. "We have to look at it until we find it."

Why are the police looking for Mike and Tony? What do you think Mike, Tony, and Kelly will find in the movie?

102

6 Bear Creek

Monday 1:30 p.m.

Look at the picture. What are Kelly, Tony, and Mike looking at? Why?

Tony and I gave in and agreed to look at the movie again with Kelly. We promised to look at it with new eyes. I wasn't hopeful. I knew what we'd find—trees and loggers cutting down trees. *Living at Bear Creek* wouldn't win any prizes as a thriller, but it was a great movie about what it really is like to live in such a remote part of the world.

There was a room full of computers at the back of the Internet café. Kelly put the DVD into a computer, and we looked at the movie, shot after shot. Then Kelly noticed a low white building through the trees and wanted to know what it was.

I explained that it was a small research place on the other side of the lake where they made medicines. "I don't think many people work there. We saw a few helicopters now and then. I'd forgotten about it, to tell you the truth."

Kelly asked if there were any better views of it. Tony hesitated for a moment and then said that he thought there were more shots of it a little farther on.

We ran the movie forward. "There!" I said.

Kelly made the picture bigger. "There's a name beside the door," she said. "I'll try and make it clearer." She hit lots of keys very fast. Then we read a name on the screen: Necross Industries.

Kelly suggested that we looked it up on the Internet.

"That's interesting," she said after a while. "They don't want anyone to know about them. Let's see if there's a back door." She typed lots of letters and numbers.

"It's very hard," she said. "Necross Industries really doesn't want anyone to know about them."

I suggested that they must have applied for permission to build their research center.

Kelly thought that was a good idea. "Government websites are always easy to get into because so many people use them." She typed some more. "Here we go," she said. "Necross Industries. Owner: Mr. N.E. Cross."

"Mr. Cross!" I cried. "We've found him."

Tony asked why Mr. Cross didn't want people to see his research center. "It's just a small building, and you can't see anything anyway. It still doesn't make sense," Tony protested.

"It's obvious that we need help," I said.

Tony suggested that we contact Teresa. "She offered to help us—she's part of the Festival," he told Kelly.

I called the number Teresa had given us.

"I thought you'd call," she said. "The police have been here asking questions about you."

I explained that we hadn't done anything wrong and asked her to believe me.

"Don't worry, I do," Teresa said.

"We think we've found out who took our movie and who wants the police to arrest us, but we still don't know why," I said. I told Teresa that the man's name was Mr. N.E. Cross and that he had a research center at Bear Creek called Necross Industries.

Teresa sounded shocked. "This is bad news! A friend of mine tried to investigate Necross Industries in California for a documentary movie a few years ago. He disappeared and we never found out what happened to him." Then she warned us not to go back to the hotel. She said that returning there was out of the question. "I'll try and find you a safe place to hide," Teresa offered. "Call me again in half an hour."

I asked if she knew who Mr. Cross was.

"No one really knows," said Teresa. "Police forces in several different countries are looking for him. But the strangest thing is that no one actually knows what he looks like, or what his real name is. There's one thing I can tell you, though," she added. "He's dangerous, very dangerous!"

Who is Mr. Cross and what is Necross Industries hiding?

7 Bear Creek

Monday 2:30 p.m.

Look at the picture. What TV show are Mike and Tony watching? What's Kelly doing?

Teresa called back half an hour later and gave us an address near Central Park.

"Go to the Movie Bookstore at this address and ask for Peter," she told us. "He'll give you a key to the apartment. I'll try and meet you there later."

We took a bus to the bookstore. Through the window I could see New Yorkers going back to their offices after lunch, shopping, and just going about their business. I felt no connection with them. It must be the feeling you get when you've been fired and everyone else carries on working normally.

Peter smiled at us, gave us the key, and told us how to get to the apartment. He didn't ask any questions, but that was to be expected.

The apartment was really close and we walked there. I don't know what I was expecting—a small apartment, lots of books and papers, and maybe some movies. For some reason, I'd thought that the owner would be someone like Teresa, but it must have belonged to a millionaire. It was not only huge, with big windows overlooking Central Park, but it was also full of beautiful modern paintings.

"Wow!" said Kelly.

There was a television with a large screen, and a laptop computer. Tony and I turned on the TV, while Kelly tried once again to get into Necross Industries' website.

We were watching the news when we heard our names again.

"Police want to talk to Mike Jovanovich and Tony McNee urgently," said the reporter. And then I saw my mother. She was being interviewed outside our house.

"Mike," she said, "if you're watching this, please contact the police immediately."

I turned off the television.

"What do you think we should do?" I asked Tony.

"I don't know," he replied. "This can't be happening to us."

But it was.

Kelly was incredibly patient. "Keep it up, Kelly!" I said. She went on working on the laptop. Tony and I talked and talked about what could be done. We just couldn't decide—nothing made any sense.

After about three hours, we still couldn't decide what to do. We were also hungry again.

Kelly found a nearby pizza place on the Internet and had some pizzas delivered.

"How's it going?" I asked her after we had eaten.

"I think I've found out how to get in," she said. "Entry is forbidden if you don't have the right password. But if you know the ropes, you can get in eventually."

Tony and I went over to the computer. The screen was full of numbers, but then, suddenly, they disappeared, and we saw the name Necross Industries.

"I'll get into the e-mails and search for your names," she said.

A few moments later we were reading dozens of e-mails about us. There was a guy called Ed writing to someone named J.

"We need to invent some false evidence so that when it is found people will think the boys have done something wrong," Ed wrote. "We don't want people to guess that we want to destroy the movie."

"Shooting the boys could be a problem," Ed wrote a day later. "People will ask too many questions. The police may visit Bear Creek. We don't want that. Yes, they could be killed in a car accident. But you know how many problems car accidents always create."

I didn't like the "always." I didn't like any of it.

"Just put some money into their bank accounts," wrote Mr. J. "Then when it is discovered by the police, they will be so busy asking about the money that the movie will be forgotten."

"It *is* the movie," I said. But what was it that we'd filmed?

We studied the DVD again, but there was nothing to be seen at Necross Industries. One or two cars had been filmed arriving, but that was all. Then suddenly I noticed a man getting out of a car.

"Can you replay that shot, Kelly?" I asked. "I think we've found the answer."

What has Mike discovered?

8 Bear Creek

Monday 6:00 p.m.

Look at the picture. Who are the people coming through the door? What are they going to say?

"It's not what we filmed, it's *who* we filmed," I said slowly. "That is Mr. Cross."

We could see him pretty clearly. He was getting out of a car and looking straight at our camera.

"That's what all this is about," I told Tony and Kelly. "You remember what Teresa said. She said that no one knew what he looked like. Well, now we do—that's why he tried to destroy our movie. He must have discovered that we were filming at Bear Creek when he went there."

"Right!" said Tony. "We must get the movie to the Festival so that everyone can see it. Once everyone knows what Mr. Cross looks like, he won't be able to do anything to us."

"But how do we get there without being arrested or killed?" I asked.

"We can e-mail the picture of Mr. Cross to the police," suggested Kelly.

"But will they believe that it's Mr. Cross?" asked Tony. "We could have just filmed anyone. How do we prove that it's Mr. Cross? Who's going to listen to us?"

"I will," said a voice behind us. The man in black was standing in the doorway.

Teresa came into the room.

"This is Jeff," she said. "He works for Canadian Security—the CSIS. He's been trying to help you, but you kept running away!"

"We didn't know who he was," I said. It all began to make sense.

"We thought the police wanted to arrest us," I went on.

"We told the police to put out a call for you," said Jeff, the CSIS man. "Because we thought it would keep Cross's men away. We knew they were following you."

"Was that one of your men at the Empire State Building?" Tony asked.

"At the Empire State Building? No. We didn't know you'd been there. That must have been one of Cross's men—you're lucky you managed to get away from him."

I felt sick. I thought of how we'd run into Macy's. He could have shot us ...

"We've figured out why they wanted to destroy our movie," said Tony. "We'd filmed Mr. Cross."

"Yes," said Jeff. "We thought it must be something like that. We've wanted to know what Mr. Cross looks like for a long time. Mr. Cross is a real mystery man. We don't know his real name or where he comes from. He was very active ten years ago—he was known as The Wolf then. We're certain he's involved in all kinds of criminal activities, but we've never been able to prove anything."

"But can't you arrest him?" asked Kelly

"We'd love to," said Jeff. "But these days, he hides behind a number of companies. We haven't been able to touch him because we have no evidence that these companies are doing anything illegal. And, amazingly, he's never been seen. He arrives from abroad in private planes and goes to remote places. By the time we get there, he's always gone. He's been one step ahead of us every time—until now ..."

"I guess we saw him because we were staying at Bear Creek for so long," I said.

"Absolutely," said Jeff. "We can't keep a man up there for months at a time. We don't have the money for that."

"But you've finally got him," said Kelly. "Look."

She showed him the picture of Mr. Cross.

"This is an excellent opportunity," said Jeff. "I must e-mail this to our offices right away. We'll need to be quick if we're going to catch him."

But at that moment we heard a noise. Someone was banging on the front door. Then there was a shot.

"It's Cross's men. They're shooting at the lock," Jeff shouted.

Can they get out of the apartment? Can they get the picture of Mr. Cross to the Festival?

9 Bear Creek

Monday 7:00 p.m.

Look at the picture. Who is the man on the screen? What happens next?

"Get out now!" shouted Jeff. "I'll follow you to the Festival as soon as I can."

"There's a staircase at the back of the apartment," said Teresa. "Quick!"

I picked up the laptop, and we ran down the back staircase. Teresa stopped a taxi and gave the driver an address.

"Are we going to the Festival?" Tony asked.

"Yes," Teresa replied. "There's a back way into the movie theater. We should be able to get in without anyone seeing us."

The taxi finally stopped on a narrow street. We ran down it, and in through a small door that we would never have noticed without Teresa. It was completely black inside.

I turned on the light, and we climbed some stone stairs and went through a series of passages until we found ourselves at the back of the movie theater. There was a small office with a computer and a telephone.

"This is Jeff's card," said Teresa. "It has his e-mail address."

"Fine," said Kelly. "Give me a few minutes and I'll send the picture of Mr. Cross to Jeff's office."

"The Festival starts in 15 minutes. Do you think you can have the movie ready by then?" Teresa asked with a worried look on her face.

"No problem," Kelly answered. She sent the e-mail and then started to connect the laptop to the movie theater equipment.

Fifteen minutes later, we were sitting in the Festival audience. Teresa walked onto the stage.

"Good evening, ladies and gentlemen," she said. "Tonight we had hoped to show you a movie by two very talented young moviemakers. Unfortunately, our copy was stolen, as were the moviemakers' own copies. The reason for this is that they happened to film this man." Behind her the face of Mr. Cross filled the screen. The audience all started to talk at once and, at the same time, two men jumped up. They had guns in their hands. As they stood up half a dozen police, including Jeff, rushed into the movie theater.

"Police! Drop your guns," shouted Jeff.

One of the men put his gun down immediately and was taken away by the police. A moment later the other man dropped his, too. In a few moments it was all over.

"Now, I'd like to introduce three very brave young people," said Teresa. Tony and Kelly and I went up on stage, and Teresa explained to the audience everything that had happened.

"Although everyone thought all the copies of the movie were stolen," Teresa finished, "this smart young woman," and she pointed to Kelly, "had made an extra copy. So now we can all enjoy *Living at Bear Creek*."

Later, Jeff told us that all of Mr. Cross's men had been arrested, though Mr. Cross had already left the country.

"But at least we know what he looks like now," said Jeff. "He won't get back into Canada so easily again."

What astonished me was that it had all happened during one day—it seemed as if we'd been in New York for ages.

Everyone wanted to see the movie now—and not just the Festival audiences. All the TV stations were asking us for interviews. It was amazing. On the last day of the Festival a producer asked Tony and me to have a meeting with him the next day.

"I'd like to discuss the idea of your making a movie about your experiences," he said.

The nightmare was over. Guess who won the prize for the best documentary! And guess who we gave the prize money to!

Bear Creek exercises

1 Monday 7:00 a.m.

1 Answer the questions.

   1 Why are Mike and Tony flying to New York?

   2 What kind of movie is *Living in Bear Creek*?

   3 What was Teresa's bad news?

   4 Who did Mike recognize in the hotel?

   5 Why did Tony call his mother?

   6 Why was Tony's mother in tears?

2 Match the verbs in list A with the words and phrases in list B. Then write the phrases.

	A	B		
1	break	a movie	**1**	*break into a house*
2	come	into a house	**2**	
3	cut	on a phone	**3**	
4	shoot	down trees	**4**	
5	spend	true	**5**	
6	turn	a long time	**6**	

3 Find words and phrases in Chapter 1 that mean the same as these phrases.

   1 try to make you believe

   2 movie about real people or events

   3 try hard to do something difficult

   4 stay alive in a difficult situation

2 Monday 9:30 a.m.

1 Look at these sentences from the story. Who do the words in **bold** refer to?

   1 "**We**'ve been waiting all night for her to call."

   2 "**She**'s not answering her cell phone."

   3 "**I**'ve been so worried."

   4 **We** couldn't have felt worse.

   5 "Yes, it's terrible," **she** agreed.

   6 So I showed **him** the copy on your computer.

   7 "I told **him** about the first detective."

   8 Neither of **us** knew what to do.

2 Complete with these prepositions.

> beside down for from on since than with

   1 Tony and Mike are older   Kelly.

   2 Kelly has been missing   yesterday.

   3 Has anyone heard   her yet?

   4 Maybe she's staying   friends.

   5 We'd been working   the movie several months.

   6 Teresa was standing   Mike and Tony.

   7 The man in black followed them   the street.

107

Bear Creek exercises

3 Monday 10:00 a.m.

1 Number the events in the right order.

   A Tony and Mike left the park. ☐
   B Tony and Mike arranged to meet Kelly. ☐
   C The man in black got into a white car. ☐
   D Tony and Mike got on a bus. ☐
   E Tony and Mike went into a park. ☐
   F Tony called his mother. ☐
   G The man in black came into the park. ☐
   H Tony and Mike borrowed clothes and skateboards. ☐
   I Kelly called Tony with some good news. ☐

2 Answer the questions.

   Why ...
   1 did Mike and Tony borrow clothes and skateboards?

   2 was Tony surprised?

   3 didn't Mike and Tony go back to their hotel?

   4 did Tony check the guidebook?

   5 did the two boys get on a bus?

   6 did Mike feel scared?

3 Find words in Chapter 3 which mean the opposite of these words and phrases.

   1 slowly
   2 in front of
   3 smart
   4 clean
   5 bottom
   6 sick
   7 arrives

4 Monday 11:30 a.m.

1 Look at these sentences from the story. Who or what do the words in **bold** refer to?

   1 We left the line, and as we **did**, so did a tall man.

   2 **We** ran across Herald Square.

   3 The tall man didn't see us leave **the store**.

   4 We could sit **there** and watch the street.

   5 "**It** doesn't need music."

   6 "This is **his** room."

   7 "**He** doesn't want anyone to see that movie."

2 Match the verbs in list A with the words and phrases in list B. Then write the phrases.

A	B	
1 carry	someone crazy	1 *carry out orders*
2 join	music	2
3 drive	something to eat	3
4 communicate	out orders	4
5 order	a line	5
6 record	with people	6

3 Find words and phrases in Chapter 4 that mean the same as these words and phrases:

   1 a very long time
   2 way into a place
   3 crowded
   4 extremely hungry
   5 destroy
   6 very nasty

108

Bear Creek exercises

5 Monday 12:30 p.m.

1 Match the beginnings with the endings.

1 Kelly thought Mike and Tony must ☐
2 Tony went to the ATM because ☐
3 Mike didn't think he had ☐
4 Tony's mother said the police ☐
5 The police believed Mike and Tony ☐
6 Mike thought Mr. Cross wanted ☐

a any money left in his bank account.
b had done something wrong.
c were looking for the two boys.
d have filmed something important.
e the police to arrest him and Tony.
f he was short of money.

2 What do the words in *italics* mean? Choose A or B.

1 "We'd *be aware of* it if we'd filmed something important."
A know   **B** understand

2 "I wish I knew, but I can't *think of* anything."
A imagine   **B** remember

3 "If only it was *that simple*."
A so clear   **B** so easy

4 "If we spent the money, we'd *never get away with it*."
A definitely be in trouble   **B** be unable to escape

5 "Something really strange is *going on*."
A happening   **B** continuing

6 "*You can't* believe that!"
A You're not allowed to   **B** Surely you don't

6 Monday 1:30 p.m.

1 Answer the questions.

Who said …?

1 "What's that building?" ....

2 "It's a small research place where they make medicines." ....

3 "Are there any better views of it?" ....

4 "I think there are some more shots of it a little farther on." ....

5 "Let's look Necross Industries up on the Internet." ....

6 "Why doesn't he want people to see his research center?" ....

7 "Please believe me." ....

8 "Don't go back to the hotel." ....

2 Match the verbs in list A with the words and phrases in list B. Then write the phrases.

	A	B		
1	apply	a movie forward	**1**	*apply for permission*
2	do	a number	**2**	
3	make	something wrong	**3**	
4	call	for permission	**4**	
5	run	shocked	**5**	
6	sound	sense	**6**	

3 Find words and phrases in Chapter 6 that mean the same as these phrases:

1 far away from everything ....
2 sometimes, but not often ....
3 didn't answer immediately ....
4 very clear ....
5 try to find out the facts ....
6 definitely not a possibility ....

Bear Creek exercises

7 Monday 2:30 p.m.

1 Number the events in the right order.

A Kelly started working on the laptop. ☐

B Mike and Tony read some worrying e-mails. ☐

C Kelly ordered some pizzas. ☐

D Mike, Tony, and Kelly went to the bookstore. ☐

E Mike and Tony watched their movie again. ☐

F Kelly got into Necross Industries' website. ☐

G Mike, Tony, and Kelly got a key to the apartment. ☐

H Mike and Tony heard their names on the TV news. ☐

2 Look at these sentences from the story. Who or what do the words in **bold** refer to?

1 "I'll try and meet you **there** later."

2 I felt no connection with **them**.

3 … but **that** was to be expected.

4 "If you're watching **this**, please contact the police immediately."

5 "We don't want **that**."

6 "**They** could be killed in a car accident."

7 "Then when **it** is discovered by the police …"

8 "Can you replay **that shot**, Kelly?"

3 Find words and phrases in Chapter 7 that mean the same as these words and phrases:

1 doing what they normally do ....

2 link ....

3 with a view over ....

4 immediately because it's important ....

5 understand the system ....

6 looked carefully at ....

8 Monday 6:00 p.m.

1 Answer the questions.

1 Why did Mr. Cross try to destroy Mike and Tony's movie?

2 The two boys had seen Jeff earlier—where and when?

3 Why had the police put out a call for Mike and Tony?

4 Why did Mike feel sick?

5 Why couldn't the CSIS arrest Mr. Cross before?

6 How had Mr. Cross managed to avoid being seen?

7 Why hadn't the CSIS sent an officer to stay at Bear Creek?

8 What was Jeff going to do just before Cross's men arrived?

2 What do the words in *italics* mean? Choose A or B.

1 We could see him *pretty clearly*.

   A quite well   **B** very obviously

2 "Who's going to *listen to* us?"

   A believe   **B** hear

3 "We haven't been able to *touch* him."

   A contact   **B** arrest

4 "*Absolutely*," said Jeff.

   A Completely.   **B** That's right.

5 He's been *one step ahead of* us."

   A smarter than   **B** faster than

6 I must e-mail this to our offices *right away*."

   A quickly   **B** immediately

3 Write sentences describing the picture on page 105.

110

Bear Creek exercises

9 Monday 7:00 p.m.

1 Match the beginnings with the endings.

1 Teresa, Kelly, and the boys left the apartment ☐

2 They managed to get into the movie theater ☐

3 Kelly sent an e-mail with the picture ☐

4 Teresa explained why the copies ☐

5 When Mr. Cross appeared on the screen, ☐

6 The police caught the two men ☐

7 Teresa introduced Mike, Tony, and Kelly ☐

8 Mike could hardly believe that ☐

9 A movie producer invited Tony and Mike ☐

a to the festival audience.

b of Mike and Tony's movie had been stolen.

c and took a taxi to the Festival.

d to have a meeting with him.

e and took them away.

f through a back door.

g everything had happened in one day.

h two gunmen in the audience jumped up.

i of Mr. Cross to Jeff's office.

2 Match the verbs in list A with the words and phrases in list B. Then write the phrases.

	A	B		
1	climb	someone a few minutes	**1**	*climb the stairs*
2	discuss	the stairs	**2**	
3	give	in the audience	**3**	
4	make	an idea	**4**	
5	sit	on the light	**5**	
6	stop	a copy	**6**	
7	turn	a taxi	**7**	

3 Find words and phrases in Chapter 9 that mean the same as these words and phrases.

1 at the same time ....

2 about six ....

3 hurried ....

4 courageous ....

5 amazed ....

6 bad dream ....

111

CLIL MEDIA STUDIES

2 Cinematography

1 Reading

Label pictures 1–7 with phrases a–g, then read the text *Cinematography: shots and angles* and check your answers.

a eye-level shot
b high-angle shot
c close-up
d long shot
e ~~low-angle shot~~
f medium shot
g reverse-angle shot

low-angle shot

Cinematography: shots and angles

Most of us have heard of the movie directors Stanley Kubrick, George Lucas, Martin Scorsese, Steven Spielberg, and Francis Ford Coppola, but how much do we know about the work of the cinematographers who have helped transform these great directors' ideas into our favorite movies? The job of a cinematographer is to choose the right camera shots, angles, and movements to create interesting scenes and sequences.

Camera shots determine what we see, based on the position of the camera. A close-up shot might draw our attention to a hand opening a door or the scared expression on somebody's face; a medium shot is often chosen to show the relationship between different characters, and a long shot to set the wider context in terms of place (for example, a distant landscape or horizon.

Camera angles tell us how to view the scene. We naturally view things in our own lives at eye level, so we tend to trust the words and emotions of a character viewed at this angle. A low-angle shot, looking up, can create a sense of power and importance, and is often used to depict villains or leaders; whereas a high-angle shot, looking down, can increase the feeling of vulnerability or weakness. A reverse-angle shot can suddenly change the perspective of what we have been looking at by seeing things through the eyes of the characters, for example, someone who is lying in the street.

2 Reading

Read the text *Cinematography: making the right moves* on page 113 and complete the table.

Technique	Camera movements	Examples of use	Effects on the audience
	camera moves from left to right		emotion or excitement
	vertically up and down	to show the side of a building as our hero climbs out of a window and escapes	suspense
	the movement of the camera closer or further from a scene		context
zooming		moving from close-ups to long shots	

4

5

Cinematography: making the right moves

Camera movement techniques are also central to how we emotionally experience a movie. "Tracking" is when the camera follows the movement, for example, of an escaping hero. It makes us feel emotionally connected to a character as we move with him/her. The speed of tracking can also affect how exciting a scene appears to us.

"Panning" immediately connects two places or characters, by moving horizontally from one to another, for example, between two people having a discussion. The speed of the pan reflects the atmosphere such as danger or relaxation.

In "tilting" the camera remains in one place, but the shot moves vertically up and down to show the side of a building as our hero climbs out of a window and escapes. Vertical movement can reflect things like social differences between characters too, and it also helps build suspense.

"Dollying" is the movement of the camera closer to or further from a scene. For example, the camera moves from a close-up of two people arguing inside a car to the long shot of the car in a deserted street, creating a context for the scene.

With "zooming," however, the camera doesn't move, but the camera lens zooms in to close-up and zooms out to long shot, focusing our attention or revealing hidden details which we hadn't noticed before.

3 Quiz

Do the quiz. Then check your answers in the texts in exercises 1 and 2.

1. Kubrick, Lucas, Scorsese, Spielberg, and Ford Coppola are famous cinematographers.
   A True   **B** False

2. Cinematographers choose the right camera shots, angles, and movements to create interesting scenes and sequences.
   A True   **B** False

3. Camera shots determine what we see based on the camera's
   A size.   **B** movement.   **C** position.

4. A close-up shot is one showing the
   A expression on somebody's face.   **B** relationship between two people.
   C wider context of a scene.

5. Camera angles tell us how to view a scene.
   A True   **B** False

6. Eye-level shots create a sense of
   A power.   **B** trust.   **C** vulnerability.

7. In order to change the point of view in a movie, you need to use a
   A high-angle shot.   **B** low-angle shot.   **C** reverse-angle shot.

8. The technique when a camera follows the movement of a character is called
   A tilting.   **B** tracking.   **C** zooming.

9. The technique which immediately connects two places or people is called
   A dollying.   **B** panning.   **C** zooming.

10. Tilting can
    A help build suspense.   **B** reflect different social class.   **C** both of these.

4 Project

Become a cinematographer! You are a famous cinematographer and you have been asked to create a storyboard for a well-known story of your choice. You can choose a fairy tale or a story you know such as *Romeo and Juliet*, but try to give the audience a different perspective on the story so that they can look at the characters in a new way. Read the following information and complete the storyboard in the template your teacher will give you for all or part of the story.

- Think of a scene from a story (for example, the balcony scene in *Romeo and Juliet*).
- Each square should contain a sketch or basic drawing of each part of the scene (don't worry if you are not very artistic—basic line drawings are fine!).
- In the space under each square, you should write the type of camera shot and movement technique.
- You can also include information about sound effects, music, or words your audience will hear.

CLIL SOCIAL SCIENCE

AFTER 4 Social and political campaigning

1 Reading

Look at the pictures of famous people and match them with the causes you think they fought for and how they did it. Then read the text *Campaigning for change: famous campaigners* and check your answers.

Who	What	How
Emmeline Pankhurst	better conditions for workers	refused to give up her seat on a bus to a white passenger
Rosa Parks	to raise money and awareness about poverty in Africa	organized a big rock concert
Bob Geldof	equal rights for black people	organized workers to join unions
Samuel Gompers	the vote for women	chained herself to the railings of 10 Downing Street

2 Vocabulary

Write these campaigning techniques under the correct heading. Then read the text *Campaigning for change: How do you do it?* on page 115 to check your answers. Can you add any more?

> banner blog body painting debate dressing up
> e-mail flash mob human chain leaflet letter
> logo making a speech movie petition picture
> postcard poster press release slide show
> social networking street campaigning symbol
> telephoning text messaging vox pop

Visual	Written	Oral
banner	*blog*	*debate*

Campaigning for change: famous campaigners

Some of the greatest social justice campaigners of all times didn't always get to see the changes they achieved, and some started campaigning almost by accident. If only they knew at the time how simple acts would change the course of history!

Let's take, for example, Emmeline Pankhurst, a campaigner for women's rights, who chained herself to the railings of the British Prime Minister's residence at 10 Downing Street in the early 1900s. She also went on hunger strike and was arrested several times. A new law giving voting rights to women was passed in the U.K. just a few weeks before Pankhurst died.

Did Rosa Parks, returning home tired one day after work in Montgomery, Alabama in the U.S. realize just how momentous her refusal to give up her seat on a bus to a white passenger would be? It led to her arrest, and to a young Martin Luther King, Jr. calling for black people to stop using the bus company and to a change in the law.

Samuel Gompers, on the other hand, was successful at organizing workers in the U.S. at the end of the 19th century to join unions to campaign for shorter hours and higher wages. He also fought for better working conditions for children.

Finally, when Irish rock star Bob Geldof decided to organize the Live Aid rock concert in 1985 to raise money and awareness about people suffering from poverty in Africa, little did he know just how successful it would be.

Campaigning for change: How do you do it?

It is possible to divide campaign strategies into three main groups. Visual campaigning includes things such as creating a campaign logo or symbol, posters and banners, movies, or photo slide shows published on the Internet. Visual stunts such as flash mobs, body painting, dressing up, or forming human chains are also examples of visual campaigning techniques. In 2005, eight million people dressed in white, wearing the symbolic white wrist band, and formed human chains around important buildings as part of the very successful *Make Poverty History* campaign. The white wrist band became a popular and powerful symbol.

An example of a flash mob is one organized by *Dancing through Disaster* in Toronto. They arranged for a large group of people to appear in a surprise location and dance, raising money for charity.

Written protests often take the form of personal letters or e-mails to important political leaders or company directors, while information or opinions are circulated on social networking sites, in Internet blogs, or by text messaging. Such methods of communication are also useful for collecting signatures on a petition expressing public support, or opposition to an issue which is then sent to a decision-maker. Many organizations distribute leaflets and press releases to inform people about campaigns. In their campaign *Save or Delete* to protect the world's forests, the environmental organization Greenpeace worked with nightclubs and youth groups to get young people to sign postcards in support of their campaign while they were out with friends.

Oral campaigning involves techniques such as street campaigning, holding a debate with different speakers, making a speech in public, recording a vox pop, or telephoning. Everybody is familiar with speeches such as Martin Luther King's "I have a dream ...," but did you know that each time there is an election, getting the public to voice their opinions on video in a vox pop is a very common way of campaigning? Another effective campaigning technique targets important participants at international conferences about economic or environmental issues. Campaigners leave messages on the answering machines of these participants, or simply symbolically block their phones in protest by lots of them calling at exactly the same time.

3 Vocabulary

Complete these sentences with the following words and phrases from the text in exercise 2. Refer back to the text if you need to.

banners   blog   debate   ~~flash mob~~   leaflets   petition   press release   vox pops

1 We'll organize a _flash mob_ at the airport, with everybody running around pretending to be airplanes to campaign against noise pollution!

2 There will be a .... on TV this evening with representatives from the two political parties.

3 People were carrying very colorful .... during the march with slogans such as "Save our planet now!" written on them.

4 The organization's .... said, "We condemn the use of child soldiers in any war."

5 If you want to support our cause, there will be an online .... for people to sign on our website.

6 A film crew will be present, recording .... of people's opinions outside the conference.

7 People will be handing out .... explaining how you can get involved with the campaign after the meeting.

8 Katy will be writing a .... throughout her trip to India, letting people know where their money is going.

4 Project

You are going to organize a campaign.

- First of all, decide what you want to campaign about. It can be a global issue, such as climate change; a national issue, such as pollution; or a smaller issue which is important to your school or community, such as new sports facilities or the amount of trash in your neighborhood.
- Next, do some research into other successful campaigns. You can look at the websites listed below for some ideas or search the Internet for past campaigns on similar issues to yours.
- Now it's time to plan your campaign strategy. Include information about:
  – the issue you are campaigning about
  – how you will let people know about your campaign (what combination of visual, written, or oral communication techniques you will use, for example, posters, blogs, speeches, etc.)
  – what you want to achieve (for example, send a signed petition to the leader of your country, hold a debate/meeting with the local authorities, get a promise from your school principal to look into ways of improving sports facilities in your school, etc.)
  – what things you will do/organize during your campaign to raise awareness and get people involved (for example, flash mob, human chain, debate, etc.).

CLIL SCIENCE

AFTER 6 Genetically Modified Organisms

1 Reading

Read the text. Then match questions a–f with paragraphs 1–6.

a How are GMOs produced?
b How will GMOs develop?
c ~~What are GMOs?~~
d What are the arguments against GMOs?
e What are the arguments in favor of GMOs?
f What are they used for?

2 Vocabulary

Match these words from the text with their definitions.

> cloning   crop   DNA
> fertilizer   genetic disorder
> herbicide   nutrient   ~~vaccine~~

1 something usually injected into the body to protect against disease
   vaccine

2 something in food that plants, animals, and people need to live and grow
   ....

3 creating an animal or plant in a laboratory in an exact copy of another using the original animal or plant's DNA
   ....

4 an illness or medical condition you inherit from your parents
   ....

5 a plant grown for food, usually on a farm
   ....

6 a natural or chemical substance added to soil to help plants grow
   ....

7 a chemical substance that contains the genetic information found in all living cells
   ....

8 a chemical for killing weeds or plants that are not wanted
   ....

Genetically Modified Organisms (GMOs)

What are GMOs?

1 All living organisms, plant or animal, have basic units called cells with a nucleus in the center. Inside the nucleus, most cells have chromosomes, which look like string. Chromosomes contain genes which carry the information inherited from the organism's parents. In a GMO (genetically modified organism), genes are changed to give a particular quality that a plant or animal would not naturally get from its parents. For example, a GM bell pepper contains DNA—the material genes are made of—from a fish. This makes the pepper survive in cold weather. Or the genes of dairy cows are modified to increase milk production.

2 GMOs are made in a scientific laboratory by combining the DNA of one organism with the DNA of another, as in the example of the pepper. GMOs are also produced by a process called cloning, which means creating an identical copy of a cell or an organism. The first cloned sheep, named Dolly, was created in 1996, but there have also been cloned pigs, horses, and dogs.

3 GMOs are used in agriculture, medical research, and to protect the environment. GM crops can resist herbicides so the farmer produces a better crop and doesn't need to spray them with the damaging chemicals used on normal crops. GM crops can also produce a poison which kills predators, but is not dangerous to humans. Some GM crops withstand extreme weather conditions or can provide extra nutrients, such as the "golden rice" developed for Asia which uses the DNA of carrots to help humans produce vitamin A. GMOs are also used to make biodegradable plastics, and to help protect endangered species such as the giant panda in China. In medicine too, scientists are using GMOs to develop drugs such as insulin. Research into the genetic modification of mosquito DNA to stop the spread of malaria is also being carried out, as well as human gene therapy to treat diseases such as cancer or genetic disorders.

4 Organizations in favor of GMOs think GM products could solve the problem of world hunger as they will lead to increased production of cheaper food which is also healthier and doesn't damage the environment. For example, according to scientific researchers, GM salmon will be cheaper to buy and will help reduce heart disease. In fact, pro-GM groups argue that GMOs are vital to medical and technological research as well as improving economies. The World Health Organization (WHO) and the United Nations Food and Agriculture Organization (FAO), also say all the GM products currently on the market are safe for humans.

116

3 Reading and writing

Complete the information about GMOs.

a Label the diagram. You can refer back to paragraph 1 in the text in exercise 1 for help.

b Complete the tables. You can refer back to paragraphs 2 and 3 in the text for help.

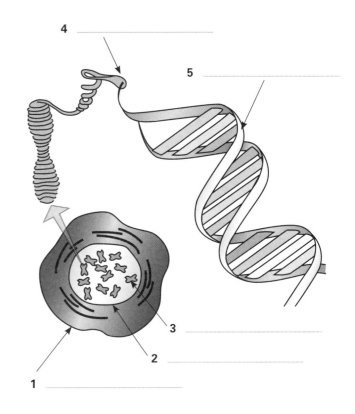

GM processes	
Process	Examples
Combining the DNA of one organism with the DNA of another	
Cloning	

GMO uses	
Area of use	Purpose
Agriculture	
Environment	
Medicine	

5 Leading environmental organizations claim GMOs will not solve the problem of world hunger, since most of the world's agriculture is not GM. They also argue that GM crops use artificial fertilizers and poisonous chemicals so they pollute the atmosphere and are dangerous to humans and animals. They also believe GMOs lead to loss of biodiversity and to climate change. In addition, they think the only people to benefit economically will be the multinational biotechnology companies, not the developing countries and not the farmers. The WHO and the FAO have also warned that GMOs should be tested for allergies and not produced to resist antibiotics.

6 Right now, GM crops are not welcomed everywhere. Around six million farmers in 16 countries, including the U.S., Australia, China, and India, grow GM crops, in particular soya beans, maize, cotton, and oilseed rape. The U.K. says it won't allow the commercial production of GM crops, and the European Union insists that they will not allow any new GM crops. In the future, GM crops will probably be more common, be more resistant to disease and extreme weather, and have additional nutrients in them. Larger animals will be produced to provide more food, and plants and animals will help produce vaccines for human diseases.

c Report what is said for or against GMOs using suitable reporting verbs. You can refer back to paragraphs 4 and 5 in the text for help. Write your answers in your notebook.

For

Organizations in favor of GMOs thought they could solve the problem of world hunger, since they will lead to increased production of cheaper food which is healthier and doesn't damage the environment.

Against

Leading environmental organizations claimed GMOs would not solve the problem of world hunger, since most of the world's agriculture was not GM.

d Complete the sentences. Use paragraph 6 in the text to help you.

1 GM crops will be _____

2 GM animals will be _____

3 GM plants and animals will help _____

4 Project

You will have a class debate about GMOs. Your teacher will tell you if you are for or against the use of GMOs. Research the arguments which support your position and prepare a two-minute talk presenting your ideas. Remember to:

- include facts, figures, and examples
- report what different organizations have said about GMOs
- try to be as convincing as possible in your argument

CLIL MUSIC
AFTER 8 Rock 'n' roll

1 Vocabulary

Match the words and phrases below with pictures.

album   concert   ~~DJ~~   electric guitar   recording studio

1 *DJ*
2 ....
3 ....
4 ....
5 ....

2 Reading

Reorder the words to form questions a–e. Then read the text and match the questions with paragraphs 1–5.

a did rock 'n' roll originate where ?
   Where did rock 'n' roll originate?

b music what the of were rock 'n' roll characteristics ?
   ....

c caused end the of roll 'n' rock what ?
   ....

d rock 'n' roll names were big who in the ?
   ....

e how rock 'n' roll culture youth did influence ?
   ....

3 Vocabulary

Match these words from the text *Rock 'n' roll* with their definitions.

~~backbeat~~   cover version   rhythm   soundtrack

1 the strongest pattern of sounds you hear as the basis of a piece of music
   backbeat

2 the music you hear in a movie
   ....

3 a regular pattern of sounds or music
   ....

4 when one artist plays or sings the song of another
   ....

Rock 'n' roll

1 *a*
An American DJ, Alan Freed, was the first to use the term "rock 'n' roll" in order to describe the music he was playing on Radio WJW in Cleveland, Ohio, in the U.S. in the 1950s. However, rock 'n' roll had its origins in black gospel, blues, and country and western music. Initially it was an underground movement—artists recorded love songs on the A-sides of their albums, but would put secret rock songs which they were not allowed to promote on the B-sides. Then Freed and others organized rock 'n' roll concerts which quickly sold out to the public and were a great success.

2 ....
In 1954 a young, good-looking, American singer came to Memphis's Sun recording studios. He was white, but he sounded black, and he was able to change the history of music. His name was Elvis Presley. Presley made rock 'n' roll popular with white audiences and let black artists such as Fats Domino, Little Richard, and Chuck Berry find a more mainstream appeal with teenagers, both white and black.

3 ....
Bill Haley & His Comets' song *Rock Around the Clock* became an instant hit when it was used as the soundtrack to *Blackboard Jungle*, a movie about youth rebellion. In fact, rock 'n' roll became a symbol for rebellion as stars such as Marlon Brando in *The Wild One* and James Dean in *Rebel Without a Cause*, were cast in the roles of rebellious youth. This led to parents, religious leaders, and the authorities criticizing the music as being dangerous and even having a demonic influence on young people. The influence of the music on young people's behavior, attitudes, fashion, and language was becoming increasingly apparent.

4 Reading

Read *Rock 'n' Roll* in exercise 1 again and complete the information.

Actors	Dance styles	Movies	Songs	Musical artists	Music styles
Marlon Brando					

5 Quiz

Read the text in exercise 1 again and do the quiz.

1 Rock 'n' roll originated in the U.S. in the 1950s.
   A True   B False

2 The expression was first used by a DJ.
   A True   B False

3 Elvis Presley appealed to white audiences.
   A True   B False

4 Bill Hayley, Marlon Brando, and James Dean were all singers.
   A True   B False

5 Parents, authorities, and religious leaders liked the influence of rock 'n' roll on young people.
   A True   B False

6 All rock 'n' roll artists wrote their own songs right from the start.
   A True   B False

7 The "jitterbug," the "sock hop," and the "twist" were famous rock 'n' roll songs.
   A True   B False

8 February 3, 1959 is known as "the day the music died."
   A True   B False

6 Project

You are a music journalist. Research and write an article for a music magazine. You can either write about one of the artists mentioned in this text (Elvis Presley, Buddy Holly, etc.), or a musical style, such as country and western or rock, or you can write about another artist or style of your choice. Remember to include:

- information about the origins of the music style
- a description of the characteristics of that musical style
- brief biographical information about an artist or group (when and where they formed, group members, important moments, etc.)
- a short discography (list of important singles and albums)
- a review of a particular single/album by the band
- your own positive or negative opinion of the group with reasons why you like or dislike it

---

4

Initially, a lot of rock 'n' roll music was cover versions of songs by other artists using the rhythms of gospel and blues. The introduction of electric guitars combined with the irregular rhythm of the backbeat led to a new and unique sound. The music also generated different energetic dance styles with names such as the "jitterbug," the "sock hop," and the "twist." By the mid 1960s, the music had become more sophisticated so that it split into the different styles which we collectively call rock music today.

5

On February 3, 1959, a plane carrying the singers Buddy Holly, J.P. Robinson (Big Bopper), and Richie Valens crashed in Iowa, in the USA, killing all three. It became known as "the day the music died." Soon after, many artists abandoned rock 'n' roll for a variety of reasons: Elvis for the army; Little Richard for the church; Jerry Lee Lewis and Chuck Berry because they were involved in scandals. Thus the great era of rock 'n' roll ended.

119

Macmillan Education
Between Towns Road, Oxford OX4 3PP
A division of Macmillan Publishers Limited
Companies and representatives throughout the world

ISBN 978-0-230-41524-9

Text © Judy Garton-Sprenger, Philip Prowse 2012
Additional text by Helena Gomm, Catrin Morris
and Catherine Smith
Design and illustration © Macmillan Publishers Limited 2012

This edition published 2012
First edition published 2008

All rights reserved; no part of this publication may be reproduced,
stored in a retrieval system, transmitted in any form, or by any
means, electronic, mechanical, photocopying, recording, or otherwise,
without the prior written permission of the publishers.

Original design by Giles Davies Design Limited
Illustrated by Adrian Barclay (Beehive Illustration Agency) p114;
Kathy Baxendale p54; Seb Camagajevac (Beehive Illustration Agency)
pp112-113; Giles Davies Design Ltd p117; Mark Davis p2; Karen
Donnelly p42; Marla Goodman pp98-106; Clive Goodyer (Beehive
Illustration Agency) p11; Tim Kahane pp52, 74*t*; Gillian Martin pp5,
93; Julian Mosedale pp30, 39, 48, 74*b*, 89; Julia Pearson pp18, 60, 62;
Simon Smith (Beehive Illustration Agency) pp24, 31, 38, 40, 50, 95;
and Harry Venning p20, 23, 46.
Cover design by Studio Montage
Cover image courtesy of Getty

The authors and publishers would like to thank the following for
permission to reproduce their photographic material:
Alamy/Stephen Bond p96(paperclip), Alamy/Ashley Cooper
p32(b), Alamy/Carolyn Jenkins p118(2), Alamy/Russell Kord
p68(b), Alamy/Melba Photo Agency p32(d), Alamy/Photoalto
p68(t), Alamy/Kumar Sriskandan p50(cr), Alamy/Charles Sturge
p78(b), Alamy/Tips Images/Tips Italia Srl a socio uncio p23; **BrandX**
p119; **Comstock Images** p118(3); **Corbis**/Caroline p32(c), Corbis/
Cultura p8, Corbis/Kevin Dodge p16, Corbis/Brownie Harris
p12, Corbis/Hulton Deutsch Collection p86(Picasso), Corbis/
Barbara Walton/epa p56(l),Corbis/Ralph White p34; **Getty Images**
p114(Samuel Gompers), Getty Images/Ty Allison p44, Getty Images/
Dirk Anschutz p76(t), Getty Images/Biddiboo p84, Getty Images/
Reggi Casagrande p36(br), Getty Images/Chabruken p92, Getty
Images/Martin Harvey p36(cl), Getty Images/Hulton Deutsch
p88, Getty Images/Frans Lemmens p14, Getty Images/Mark Scott
p36(tr), Getty Images/Tetra Images p78(t), Getty Images/Time &
Life Pictures p114(Rosa Parkes), Getty Images/Norbert Wu p28;

Harvard-Smithsonian Center for Astrophysics/David A Aguilar
(CfA) p26; **Image Source** p90; **Kobal**/Selznick/MGM p17, Kobal/
Universal p6; **Kyle Macdonald** p96(house); **Macmillan** p118(1); **Mary
Evans Picture Library** pp50(t),80, Mary Evans Picture Library/The
Woman's Library p114(Emmeline Pankhurst); **Rex Features**/Canadian
Press p72, Rex Features/Nick Cunard p4, Rex Features/Jenny Davies
p86(Akio Morita), Rex Features/Everett Collection p86(Walt Disney),
Rex Features/Sipa Press p32(a), Rex Features/Sipa Press p86(Michael
Jordan), Rex Features/Startraks Photo p119, Rex Features/Rob
Taggart/Associated Newspapers p114(Bob Geldof); **Robert Harding
Picture Library**/age footstock p66; **Science Photo Library** p76(b);
Stockbyte p116, **SWNS** p56(r).

The author and publishers are grateful for permission to reprint the
following copyright material:
Page 4: Extract from *'Cyclean'* by Alex Gadsden copyright © Alex
Gadsden www.cyclean.biz/about.html;
Page 87: Extract from 'A Genius Explains' by Richard Johnson
copyright © Richard Johnson, first published in The Guardian
12.02.05, reprinted by permission of the author;
Page 20: Extract from *'Stories for Thinking'* by Robert Fisher copyright
© Robert Fisher 1996, reprinted by permission of the author;
Page 64: Extract from *'Down Under'* by Bill Bryson, published by
Black Swan. Reprinted by permission of The Random House Group
Ltd. and Greene & Heaton;
Page 72: Extract from *'In Africa on Wheels'* by Gordon Rattray
copyright © Gordon Rattray, first published in Forward Magazine
February 2005, reprinted by permission of the author;
Page 56: Extract from 'Lek' Chailert' by Luke Duggleby copyright
© Luke Duggleby first published in LIV Magazine Issue 3, 2006,
reprinted by permission of the author;
Page 72: Extract from *'Handcycling'* by Piers Stone copyright © Piers
Stone, first published in Forward Magazine February 2006, reprinted
by permission of the author;
Page 77: Dr Catherine Walker of the Institute of Education,
University of London has given approval for Macmillan Education
to use material from *'Code of Practice for Citing Sources and Avoiding
Plagiarism'*, copyright © 2006;
Page 76: Extract on *Dr Lynne Elkin* courtesy of WGBH Boston.
Copyright © 2003 WGBH Educational Foundation.

These materials may contain links for third-party websites. We have
no control over, and are not responsible for, the contents of such
third-party websites. Please use care when accessing them.

Although we have tried to trace and contact copyright holders before
publication, in some cases this has not been possible. If contacted
we will be pleased to rectify any errors or omissions at the earliest
opportunity.

Printed and bound in Thailand

2016   2015   2014   2013   2012
10 9 8 7 6 5 4 3 2 1